Marketing for Car Dealerships and AI

Richard Halbe

Introduction

(table of contents at the end of the book)
Purpose of the Book

The automotive industry is in a state of constant evolution, driven by technological advancements, changing consumer behaviors, and the increasing integration of digital tools. For car dealerships, staying competitive means not only understanding these changes but also effectively leveraging new technologies to meet consumer demands and enhance operational efficiency. This book aims to serve as a comprehensive guide for car dealership professionals, from marketing managers to sales executives, who are eager to harness the power of Artificial Intelligence (AI) to elevate their marketing strategies, improve customer experiences, and drive sales growth.

Why Car Dealerships Need AI

In an era where personalization, efficiency, and data-driven decision-making are paramount, AI offers car dealerships an unparalleled opportunity to revolutionize their marketing efforts. AI can transform how dealerships understand and engage with customers, streamline operations, and optimize every facet of the customer journey, from initial contact to post-purchase follow-up. Whether it's through personalized marketing messages, predictive analytics for better inventory management, or AI-driven customer service tools, the integration of AI into dealership marketing strategies is no longer a luxury—it's a necessity for those looking to maintain a competitive edge.

Overview of What Readers Will Learn

Readers of this book will gain a solid understanding of both the fundamentals and advanced concepts of marketing within the context of the car dealership industry. Part 1 of the book will cover the basics of car dealership marketing, focusing on understanding market trends, consumer behavior, and foundational digital marketing strategies. Part 2 will introduce readers to the transformative potential of AI in marketing, exploring how data analysis, chatbots, and AI-driven advertising can enhance customer insights and engagement. Part 3 will delve into advanced applications of AI, including dynamic pricing, virtual showrooms, and predictive maintenance, demonstrating how these technologies can revolutionize dealership operations. Finally, Part 4 will look towards the future, discussing emerging AI trends, ethical considerations, and the skills required to build an AI-ready team.

Part 1: The Basics of Car Dealership Marketing

Chapter 1: Understanding the Automotive Market

Market Trends and Consumer Behavior

The automotive market has undergone significant transformations over the past decade, driven by various factors, including technological innovations, regulatory changes, and shifting consumer preferences. To successfully market to today's car buyers, dealerships must have a deep understanding of these trends and the underlying consumer behaviors that drive them.

Key Market Trends

The Rise of Electric Vehicles (EVs)

With increasing concerns about environmental sustainability and rising fuel prices, the demand for electric vehicles has surged. Automakers are investing heavily in EV technology, expanding their electric offerings, and setting ambitious targets for phasing out internal combustion engine (ICE) vehicles. For dealerships, this shift means adjusting inventory, marketing strategies, and sales approaches to cater to environmentally conscious consumers who are interested in electric and hybrid vehicles.

The Shift Towards Online Car Shopping

The traditional car buying process, which often involved multiple visits to dealerships, is being replaced by online research and shopping. Consumers now prefer to start their car-buying journey online, comparing prices, reading reviews, and even completing transactions without ever setting foot in a dealership. Dealerships must therefore focus on improving their online presence, optimizing their websites for search engines, and providing detailed, transparent information about their inventory.

The Impact of the Sharing Economy

Services like Uber and Lyft, along with car-sharing platforms, are changing the way people think about car ownership. Younger generations, particularly millennials and Gen Z, are less likely to purchase cars compared to older generations, opting instead for shared mobility solutions. This trend presents both a challenge and an opportunity for dealerships: they must rethink their traditional sales models and explore partnerships with ride-sharing and car-sharing services to tap into this market.

Increased Focus on Sustainability

Beyond the shift to electric vehicles, there is a broader push towards sustainability in the automotive industry. Consumers are increasingly concerned about the environmental impact of their purchases, and this extends to the types of vehicles they drive. Dealerships can appeal to these environmentally conscious buyers by highlighting the sustainability features of their vehicles, offering eco-friendly maintenance options, and promoting corporate social responsibility initiatives.

Technological Advancements in Vehicles

Modern vehicles are equipped with advanced technologies such as autonomous driving features, connected car services, and enhanced infotainment systems. These features not only improve the driving experience but also serve as major selling points. Dealerships need to stay informed about the latest automotive technologies and be prepared to educate potential customers about the benefits of these advancements.

Understanding Consumer Behavior

Research-Driven Decision Making

Today's consumers are more informed than ever before. With the vast amount of information available online, car buyers typically spend a significant amount of time researching vehicles before making a purchase decision. They compare prices, read reviews, watch video tutorials, and seek out expert opinions. Dealerships can leverage this behavior by providing comprehensive and accurate information on their websites, engaging in content marketing, and building trust through transparency.

Demand for Personalization

Consumers expect personalized experiences in all aspects of their lives, including car shopping. They want vehicles that meet their specific needs and preferences, as well as tailored interactions with sales and service staff. Utilizing customer data to provide personalized recommendations, offers, and follow-up communications can significantly enhance the customer experience and increase loyalty.

Value-Oriented Purchasing

While price remains a critical factor in car buying decisions, consumers are increasingly looking for value beyond just the sticker price. They consider factors such as fuel efficiency, maintenance costs, and resale value. Dealerships should focus on communicating the long-term value of their vehicles, highlighting features that save money over time, and offering financing options that make purchasing more affordable.

Preference for a Hassle-Free Experience

The car buying process can be stressful and time-consuming, which is why many consumers appreciate a streamlined, hassle-free experience. Dealerships that can offer efficient and straightforward purchasing processes, whether through online platforms or in-person interactions, will have a competitive advantage. Implementing tools such as online financing applications, home delivery options, and virtual test drives can help simplify the buying process.

Traditional vs. Digital Marketing in Car Dealerships

Traditional Marketing Approaches

Traditional marketing methods, such as print ads, radio spots, television commercials, and billboards, have been the mainstay of car dealership marketing for decades. These methods can still be effective, particularly for reaching older demographics or establishing a broad local presence. Traditional marketing helps build brand recognition and can drive foot traffic to the dealership. However, these methods often lack the precision and measurability of digital marketing, making it difficult to track ROI and target specific customer segments.

The Shift to Digital Marketing

Digital marketing has revolutionized the way car dealerships reach potential customers. The ability to target specific audiences, measure campaign effectiveness, and engage with customers in real-time makes digital marketing an essential component of a successful marketing strategy. Key digital marketing tactics for car dealerships include:

Search Engine Optimization (SEO)

SEO is crucial for ensuring that a dealership's website appears in search results when potential customers are looking for cars. By optimizing their websites for relevant keywords, creating high-quality content, and building backlinks, dealerships can improve their visibility and attract more organic traffic.

Content Marketing

Providing valuable content, such as blog posts, videos, and infographics, can help establish a dealership as a trusted source of information. Content marketing not only aids in SEO efforts but also helps educate potential customers, builds trust, and guides them through the sales funnel.

Social Media Marketing

Platforms like Facebook, Instagram, and Twitter offer powerful tools for engaging with potential customers, promoting vehicles, and building a community around the dealership brand. Social media allows for targeted advertising, real-time customer interaction, and the sharing of customer testimonials and success stories.

Email Marketing and CRM Integration

Email marketing remains a highly effective way to nurture leads and maintain relationships with past customers. Integrating email campaigns with Customer Relationship Management (CRM) systems enables dealerships to send personalized messages, track customer interactions, and automate follow-up communications based on customer behavior.

Online Advertising

Pay-per-click (PPC) advertising, display ads, and social media ads allow dealerships to reach specific demographics, remarket to website visitors, and promote special offers. The ability to target ads based on user behavior, interests, and location makes online advertising a cost-effective way to drive traffic and generate leads.

Chapter 2: The Customer Journey in Automotive Sales

Understanding the customer journey is crucial for car dealerships aiming to provide a seamless and satisfying experience for potential buyers. The customer journey in automotive sales typically consists of three main stages: Awareness, Consideration, and Decision. Each stage presents unique opportunities for dealerships to engage with customers, build relationships, and guide them towards making a purchase.

Awareness Stage

Understanding the Awareness Stage

The Awareness stage is the first point of contact a customer has with a dealership or a brand. During this stage, potential customers recognize a need or desire for a new vehicle, but they are not yet familiar with specific brands, models, or dealerships. Their primary goal is to gather information and explore options. Effective marketing strategies in this stage focus on visibility and education, helping potential customers become aware of the dealership and the vehicles it offers.

Strategies for the Awareness Stage

Content Marketing

Creating valuable, informative content is a powerful way to attract attention during the Awareness stage. Blog posts, videos, and guides that answer common car-buying questions, explain the benefits of different types of vehicles (e.g., electric vs. gasoline), or provide tips for first-time buyers can draw traffic to the dealership's website and establish the dealership as a trusted resource. Content should be optimized for search engines to ensure it reaches a broad audience.

Social Media Presence

Social media platforms are ideal for building brand awareness and engaging with a wide audience. Regular posts that showcase new inventory, share customer testimonials, highlight dealership events, and provide educational content can help capture the interest of potential customers. Paid social media advertising can further enhance visibility by targeting specific demographics based on location, interests, and online behavior.

Search Engine Optimization (SEO)

Ensuring the dealership's website is optimized for relevant keywords is critical for appearing in search results when potential customers are looking for information about cars. Local SEO is particularly important, as many customers will search for dealerships in their area. Using location-specific keywords, claiming and optimizing the dealership's Google My Business listing, and acquiring positive customer reviews can help improve local search rankings.

Online Advertising

Pay-per-click (PPC) advertising and display ads can effectively reach potential customers who are in the early stages of their car-buying journey. Ads targeting relevant keywords and phrases can drive traffic to the dealership's website, where visitors can learn more about available vehicles and services.

Consideration Stage

Understanding the Consideration Stage

During the Consideration stage, potential customers have moved from simply being aware of their need for a vehicle to actively researching their options. They are comparing different brands, models, and dealerships, and are seeking out detailed information to help them make an informed decision. At this point, customers are looking for reasons to choose one option over another, making it essential for dealerships to differentiate themselves and provide compelling value propositions.

Strategies for the Consideration Stage

Product Information and Comparisons

Providing detailed information about each vehicle in the dealership's inventory, including specifications, features, pricing, and comparisons with competing models, is crucial. Interactive tools such as vehicle comparison charts, virtual showrooms, and 360-degree video tours can enhance the online shopping experience, making it easier for customers to visualize and compare options.

Customer Reviews and Testimonials

Positive reviews and testimonials from satisfied customers can significantly influence potential buyers during the Consideration stage. Displaying reviews on the dealership's website, sharing customer success stories on social media, and encouraging happy customers to leave feedback on review platforms like Google and Yelp can build trust and credibility.

Lead Magnets and Offers

Offering lead magnets, such as downloadable buying guides, checklists, or special reports, can capture the attention of potential customers and encourage them to provide their contact information. Additionally, special offers, such as limited-time discounts, financing deals, or trade-in incentives, can motivate customers to choose a specific dealership over others.

Personalized Follow-Up

Implementing a robust Customer Relationship Management (CRM) system allows dealerships to track customer interactions and preferences, enabling personalized follow-up communications. Automated emails, targeted offers, and personalized recommendations can keep potential customers engaged and guide them towards making a purchase decision.

Decision Stage

Understanding the Decision Stage

In the Decision stage, potential customers are ready to make a purchase. They have narrowed down their choices and are considering final factors such as price, dealership reputation, and overall buying experience. This is the stage where the dealership needs to provide reassurance, address any remaining concerns, and make the buying process as smooth and straightforward as possible.

Strategies for the Decision Stage

Transparent Pricing and Financing Options

Transparency is key to building trust with customers ready to make a decision. Clearly displaying pricing information, explaining financing options, and offering online payment calculators can help customers feel more confident in their purchase. Being upfront about all costs, including taxes, fees, and optional extras, can prevent misunderstandings and build long-term trust.

Exceptional Customer Service

The quality of customer service can be a deciding factor for many buyers. Providing responsive, helpful, and knowledgeable service, both online and in-person, can significantly impact the final decision. Training sales staff to listen to customer needs, answer questions accurately, and offer personalized recommendations can enhance the overall buying experience.

Virtual Showrooms and Online Transactions

The ability to complete transactions online is becoming increasingly important. Offering virtual showroom tours, online vehicle reservations, and the option to complete paperwork digitally can streamline the buying process and appeal to customers who prefer a more convenient and contactless experience. Additionally, offering home delivery or pickup services can provide added convenience.

Handling Objections and Building Trust

Addressing any last-minute objections or concerns is critical during the Decision stage. Sales staff should be trained to handle common objections, such as concerns about price, financing terms, or vehicle reliability, with confidence and empathy. Providing reassurance through warranties, return policies, and after-sales support can help build trust and close the sale.

Importance of Customer Experience

Throughout the entire customer journey, providing an exceptional customer experience is paramount. Every interaction, from the first visit to the dealership's website to post-purchase follow-up, contributes to the customer's overall perception of the dealership. Prioritizing customer experience can lead to higher customer satisfaction, repeat business, and positive word-of-mouth referrals.

Consistency Across Channels

Whether customers are interacting with the dealership online, over the phone, or in-person, the experience should be consistent. Ensuring that all touchpoints reflect the dealership's brand values, tone, and quality of service can create a cohesive and trustworthy customer journey.

Listening to Customer Feedback

Actively seeking and responding to customer feedback is essential for continuous improvement. Surveys, reviews, and direct feedback can provide valuable insights into what customers value and where there may be opportunities to enhance the experience. Addressing feedback promptly and making visible improvements shows customers that their opinions matter.

Investing in Customer Relationship Management (CRM)

A robust CRM system is a valuable tool for managing customer interactions, tracking leads, and personalizing communications. By maintaining detailed records of customer preferences, past interactions, and purchase history, dealerships can tailor their approach to meet individual needs and build stronger relationships.

Post-Purchase Engagement

The customer journey doesn't end with the sale. Follow-up communications, such as thank-you emails, maintenance reminders, and invitations to dealership events, can help maintain a positive relationship and encourage repeat business. Offering exceptional after-sales support and addressing any issues that arise promptly can further enhance customer loyalty.

Chapter 3: Branding and Positioning

In an increasingly competitive automotive market, a strong brand identity is essential for car dealerships to stand out and attract customers. Branding goes beyond logos and slogans; it encompasses the overall perception that customers have of a dealership, including its reputation, values, and the emotional connections it fosters. Effective branding and positioning strategies help create a unique identity, differentiate the dealership from competitors, and build lasting relationships with customers.

Building a Strong Brand Identity

Understanding Brand Identity

Brand identity is the combination of visual elements, messaging, and values that define how a brand is perceived by the public. For car dealerships, a strong brand identity can communicate trust, quality, and a commitment to customer satisfaction. It sets the tone for all interactions and plays a crucial role in shaping the customer experience.

Key Components of Brand Identity

Brand Vision and Mission

The brand vision is a long-term aspirational goal that reflects what the dealership aims to achieve, while the mission is a statement of purpose that outlines how the dealership intends to reach that vision. Together, these statements provide direction and serve as a foundation for all branding efforts. A clear and compelling vision and mission can inspire both employees and customers, creating a sense of purpose and alignment.

Brand Values

Brand values are the principles and beliefs that guide a dealership's actions and decisions. These values should resonate with both the dealership's team and its customers. Common values in the automotive industry include trustworthiness, customer focus, innovation, and sustainability. By consistently demonstrating these values in every aspect of the business, dealerships can build credibility and foster trust with their customers.

Visual Identity

The visual identity includes all the visual elements associated with the brand, such as the logo, color scheme, typography, and design style. A cohesive visual identity helps create recognition and memorability. For example, a modern, sleek logo might convey innovation and forward-thinking, while a classic, timeless design might suggest reliability and tradition. The visual identity should be consistently applied across all marketing materials, from the website and social media profiles to in-store signage and promotional items.

Brand Voice and Messaging

The brand voice is the tone and style of communication used by the dealership, while messaging refers to the key messages conveyed to the audience. A consistent brand voice and clear messaging help establish the dealership's personality and connect with customers on an emotional level. Whether the tone is friendly and approachable or professional and authoritative, it should align with the brand's values and appeal to the target audience.

Customer Experience

The customer experience is a critical component of brand identity. Every interaction, from the initial website visit to after-sales support, contributes to how customers perceive the brand. A positive, consistent customer experience reinforces the dealership's brand identity and can lead to increased customer loyalty and advocacy. Investing in training for employees, implementing customer-friendly policies, and actively seeking feedback are ways to enhance the customer experience and strengthen the brand.

Differentiating Your Dealership

The Importance of Differentiation

In a market where customers have numerous options to choose from, differentiation is key to standing out. Differentiation involves highlighting the unique aspects of the dealership that set it apart from competitors. These differentiators can be based on various factors, including product offerings, pricing, customer service, location, or unique selling propositions (USPs).

Strategies for Differentiation

Unique Selling Propositions (USPs)

A USP is a clear and compelling reason why customers should choose one dealership over another. It answers the question, "What makes this dealership unique?" Identifying and promoting a strong USP can give a dealership a competitive edge. Examples of USPs in the automotive industry include offering a no-haggle pricing policy, specializing in a specific type of vehicle (e.g., luxury, electric, or certified pre-owned), providing a lifetime warranty, or offering superior customer service.

Focus on Customer Service Excellence

Exceptional customer service can be a powerful differentiator. By creating a welcoming and supportive environment, being attentive to customer needs, and going above and beyond to resolve issues, dealerships can build a reputation for outstanding service. Implementing customer service training programs, setting clear service standards, and recognizing employees who excel in customer interactions can help cultivate a customer-centric culture.

Leveraging Technology and Innovation

Adopting new technologies and innovative practices can set a dealership apart from its competitors. Examples include offering virtual reality (VR) or augmented reality (AR) showroom experiences, implementing AI-driven tools for personalized recommendations, or using data analytics to enhance customer insights and optimize marketing efforts. By embracing technology, dealerships can offer unique, modern, and convenient experiences that appeal to tech-savvy customers.

Community Involvement and Social Responsibility

Building a strong connection with the local community can differentiate a dealership and enhance its brand reputation. Participating in or sponsoring community events, supporting local charities, and engaging in environmentally sustainable practices demonstrate a commitment to the community and social responsibility. These efforts not only attract customers who value corporate social responsibility but also create positive word-of-mouth and strengthen the dealership's image.

Creating a Memorable Dealership Experience

The physical environment of the dealership can also serve as a differentiator. Creating a comfortable, inviting, and memorable space can leave a lasting impression on customers. Considerations might include modern showroom designs, interactive displays, comfortable waiting areas, and amenities such as free Wi-Fi or refreshments. A unique and pleasant dealership environment can enhance the overall customer experience and set the dealership apart.

Branding in the Digital Age

Online Presence and Reputation Management

In today's digital world, a dealership's online presence is a crucial aspect of its brand identity. Customers often form their first impressions based on online interactions, making it essential for dealerships to manage their online reputation proactively.

Website Design and User Experience

The dealership's website is often the first point of contact for potential customers. A well-designed, user-friendly website that reflects the dealership's brand identity can create a positive first impression. Important considerations include easy navigation, fast loading times, mobile responsiveness, and clear calls to action. The website should also provide comprehensive information about available vehicles, pricing, and services.

Social Media Engagement

Social media platforms offer opportunities for dealerships to engage with customers, showcase their brand personality, and build a community of loyal followers. Consistent, authentic engagement on social media can enhance brand visibility and foster customer relationships. Dealerships should use social media to share valuable content, respond to customer inquiries, and participate in conversations related to the automotive industry.

Online Reviews and Testimonials

Online reviews play a significant role in shaping a dealership's reputation. Encouraging satisfied customers to leave positive reviews on platforms like Google, Yelp, and Facebook can boost the dealership's credibility and attract new customers. It's also important to respond to both positive and negative reviews professionally and promptly, demonstrating a commitment to customer satisfaction and continuous improvement.

Content Marketing and Thought Leadership

Publishing valuable, informative content can establish a dealership as a thought leader in the automotive industry. Blog posts, videos, podcasts, and webinars that address common questions, provide expert insights, and offer helpful tips can attract and engage potential customers. Content marketing not only drives traffic to the dealership's website but also builds trust and positions the dealership as a knowledgeable and reliable resource.

Measuring Brand Success

Key Performance Indicators (KPIs)

To assess the effectiveness of branding efforts, dealerships should track key performance indicators (KPIs) that reflect brand awareness, customer perception, and overall brand strength. Common KPIs for measuring brand success include:

Brand Awareness

Metrics such as website traffic, social media reach, and search engine rankings can indicate the level of brand awareness. Surveys and market research can also provide insights into how well the dealership is recognized and perceived by the target audience.

Customer Satisfaction and Loyalty

Customer satisfaction surveys, Net Promoter Score (NPS), and customer retention rates are valuable indicators of how customers feel about the dealership and their likelihood of returning or recommending it to others.

Online Reputation

Monitoring online reviews, ratings, and social media sentiment can provide insights into the dealership's reputation and how it is perceived by customers. Tracking changes in online reviews over time can help identify areas for improvement and measure the impact of reputation management efforts.

Sales and Market Share

Ultimately, the success of branding efforts is reflected in sales performance and market share. Tracking sales data, market share growth, and customer acquisition costs can provide a clear picture of how well the dealership is attracting and retaining customers.

Conclusion

A strong brand identity and effective positioning are essential for car dealerships to thrive in a competitive market. By defining a clear brand vision, differentiating through unique selling propositions, leveraging technology, and delivering exceptional customer experiences, dealerships can create a powerful brand that resonates with customers and drives long-term success. In the digital age, managing online presence and reputation is equally important, ensuring that the dealership's brand is consistently represented and positively perceived across all channels.

Chapter 4: Digital Marketing Fundamentals

Digital marketing has become a cornerstone of successful car dealership strategies. As more consumers turn to online platforms to research, compare, and purchase vehicles, dealerships must adopt comprehensive digital marketing tactics to attract, engage, and convert potential buyers. This chapter explores the essential components of digital marketing for car dealerships, including search engine optimization (SEO), content marketing, social media strategies, and email marketing. By mastering these fundamentals, dealerships can effectively reach their target audience, drive traffic to their websites, and increase sales.

SEO and Content Marketing

Understanding SEO

Search Engine Optimization (SEO) is the practice of optimizing a website to rank higher in search engine results pages (SERPs), thereby increasing organic traffic. For car dealerships, SEO is crucial because it helps potential customers find the dealership when searching for vehicles, services, or automotive information online. A well-optimized website can improve visibility, enhance credibility, and attract high-quality leads.

Key SEO Strategies for Car Dealerships

Keyword Research

The foundation of any SEO strategy is keyword research. Identifying the right keywords—terms and phrases that potential customers use when searching for cars or related services—is essential for driving relevant traffic to the dealership's website. Tools like Google Keyword Planner, SEMrush, and Ahrefs can help identify popular and relevant keywords. Dealerships should focus on a mix of high-volume, competitive keywords (e.g., "new cars for sale") and long-tail keywords that are more specific and less competitive (e.g., "used SUVs in [city name]"). Including location-based keywords is particularly important for local SEO, as many customers search for dealerships near them.

On-Page Optimization

On-page SEO involves optimizing individual web pages to rank higher and earn more relevant traffic. Key on-page elements include:

- **Title Tags and Meta Descriptions**: These HTML elements appear in search results and should include relevant keywords and compelling descriptions to encourage clicks.

- **Headings (H1, H2, H3 tags)**: Using headings to structure content makes it easier for search engines to understand the page's hierarchy and for users to navigate.

- **URL Structure**: URLs should be short, descriptive, and include relevant keywords. Avoid using long, complex URLs with unnecessary parameters.

- **Content Quality**: High-quality, informative, and engaging content is critical for SEO success. Pages should provide value to users, answer their questions, and include relevant keywords naturally.

Local SEO

Local SEO focuses on optimizing a website to attract local customers. Key strategies include:

- **Google My Business (GMB)**: Claiming and optimizing the dealership's GMB listing is essential for appearing in local search results and Google Maps. Ensure that the listing includes accurate information, such as the dealership's name, address, phone number, website, and business hours. Encourage satisfied customers to leave positive reviews on the GMB listing, as reviews impact local search rankings.

- **Local Citations**: Ensure the dealership's name, address, and phone number (NAP) are consistent across all online directories and platforms, such as Yelp, Yellow Pages, and automotive directories. Consistency helps search engines verify the dealership's location and improve local search visibility.

Technical SEO

Technical SEO involves optimizing the website's infrastructure to improve its crawlability, indexability, and performance. Important technical SEO aspects include:

- **Website Speed**: Fast-loading websites provide a better user experience and are favored by search engines. Optimize images, use a content delivery network (CDN), and minimize JavaScript and CSS files to improve site speed.

- **Mobile-Friendliness**: With a significant number of users accessing websites via mobile devices, having a mobile-friendly design is crucial. Use responsive design to ensure the website looks and functions well on all devices.

- **Secure Website (HTTPS)**: Security is a ranking factor for Google. Ensure the website uses HTTPS encryption to protect user data and build trust.

Content Marketing for Car Dealerships

Content marketing involves creating and sharing valuable content to attract and engage a target audience. For car dealerships, content marketing can position the dealership as an industry expert, build trust with potential customers, and drive traffic to the website.

Blog Posts and Articles

Regularly publishing blog posts and articles on the dealership's website can improve SEO, drive traffic, and establish the dealership as a trusted resource. Topics can include car-buying tips, maintenance advice, comparisons of different models, and industry news. Content should be informative, engaging, and optimized with relevant keywords. Incorporating visuals, such as images and videos, can enhance the appeal of the content.

Video Content

Video is a highly engaging format that can capture the attention of potential customers. Dealerships can create videos showcasing new inventory, providing virtual tours of the showroom, or offering how-to guides on car maintenance. Videos can be shared on the dealership's website, YouTube channel, and social media platforms to reach a wider audience.

Infographics

Infographics are visual representations of information and can be an effective way to convey complex data in a simple and engaging format. Dealerships can create infographics on topics such as the car-buying process, fuel efficiency comparisons, or the benefits of regular maintenance. Infographics are highly shareable and can drive traffic to the website when shared on social media or embedded in blog posts.

E-books and Guides

Offering downloadable e-books or guides on topics such as "The Ultimate Guide to Buying a Car" or "How to Choose the Right Vehicle for Your Family" can capture leads by requiring users to provide their contact information in exchange for the content. These lead magnets can nurture potential customers and move them further down the sales funnel.

Social Media Strategies

The Role of Social Media in Car Dealership Marketing

Social media platforms are powerful tools for car dealerships to connect with potential customers, showcase inventory, and build brand loyalty. With the ability to reach a broad audience, engage in real-time conversations, and share a variety of content types, social media is an essential component of a dealership's digital marketing strategy.

Key Social Media Platforms for Car Dealerships

Facebook

Facebook is one of the most popular social media platforms and offers extensive targeting options for advertising. Dealerships can use Facebook to share updates, post photos and videos of inventory, host live events, and engage with customers through comments and messages. Facebook Ads can target users based on demographics, interests, and behaviors, making it an effective platform for reaching potential car buyers.

Instagram

Instagram's visual nature makes it ideal for showcasing vehicles and creating a visually appealing brand presence. Dealerships can use Instagram to post high-quality images and videos of new arrivals, behind-the-scenes content, and customer testimonials. Instagram Stories and Reels offer additional opportunities for engagement through short, engaging video content. Using relevant hashtags can increase the visibility of posts and attract a wider audience.

X (former Twitter)

X is a platform for real-time communication and can be used to share quick updates, industry news, and promotional offers. Engaging with followers through retweets, replies, and mentions can build a sense of community and keep the dealership top-of-mind. X Ads can be used to promote specific tweets, drive website traffic, or generate leads.

LinkedIn

While LinkedIn is primarily a professional networking platform, it can be useful for B2B marketing, such as fleet sales or partnerships with local businesses. Dealerships can use LinkedIn to share industry insights, company news, and connect with other businesses or professionals in the automotive industry.

YouTube

YouTube is a leading platform for video content and offers opportunities for dealerships to showcase their inventory, provide virtual tours, and share educational content. Creating a YouTube channel allows dealerships to upload videos, create playlists, and engage with viewers through comments. YouTube Ads can reach a wide audience and drive traffic to the dealership's website or specific video content.

Social Media Content Ideas

Inventory Showcases

Posting photos and videos of new and featured vehicles can generate interest and drive inquiries. Highlighting key features, pricing, and special promotions can encourage potential buyers to visit the dealership or request more information.

Customer Testimonials

Sharing positive experiences from satisfied customers can build trust and credibility. Testimonials can be shared as text posts, video interviews, or images of happy customers with their new vehicles.

Behind-the-Scenes Content

Providing a behind-the-scenes look at the dealership's operations, staff, and events can humanize the brand and create a sense of transparency. Content ideas include employee spotlights, service department tours, or footage from dealership events.

Promotional Offers and Contests

Announcing special offers, discounts, or limited-time promotions can drive engagement and sales. Running contests or giveaways on social media can increase followers and encourage participation.

Educational Content

Sharing tips, advice, and informative content can position the dealership as an expert in the automotive industry. Topics might include car maintenance tips, financing advice, or explanations of new vehicle technologies.

Email Marketing and CRM Integration

The Power of Email Marketing

Email marketing remains one of the most effective digital marketing channels for car dealerships. It allows dealerships to communicate directly with potential and existing customers, provide personalized content, and nurture leads through the sales funnel. With a well-segmented email list and targeted messaging, dealerships can drive engagement, build relationships, and increase sales.

Building an Email List

Lead Capture Forms

Adding lead capture forms to the dealership's website, such as newsletter sign-ups, contact forms, or downloadable content offers, can help build an email list. These forms should be easy to find and simple to complete. Offering incentives, such as discounts or exclusive content, can encourage visitors to provide their contact information.

In-Store Sign-Ups

Encouraging customers to sign up for email updates during their visit to the dealership can expand the email list. Sales and service staff can ask customers if they would like to receive notifications about special offers, events, or vehicle maintenance reminders.

Social Media Promotions

Promoting email sign-ups on social media platforms can drive traffic to lead capture forms and increase subscriptions. Running social media contests or offering exclusive content to email subscribers can incentivize sign-ups.

Email Content Strategies

Newsletters

Regular newsletters keep customers informed about dealership news, upcoming events, new inventory, and industry updates.

Newsletters should be visually appealing, easy to read, and provide valuable information to keep subscribers engaged.

Promotional Emails

Sending targeted promotional emails about special offers, discounts, or financing options can drive immediate action. Personalizing emails based on the recipient's interests, preferences, or past interactions can increase relevance and effectiveness.

Follow-Up Emails

Automated follow-up emails can nurture leads and keep potential customers engaged. Examples include sending a thank-you email after a test drive, providing additional information after an inquiry, or reminding customers about upcoming service appointments.

Customer Retention Emails

Retaining existing customers is just as important as acquiring new ones. Sending personalized emails with service reminders, birthday greetings, or loyalty rewards can strengthen customer relationships and encourage repeat business.

Integrating CRM with Email Marketing

A Customer Relationship Management (CRM) system helps dealerships manage customer interactions, track leads, and automate email marketing campaigns. Integrating CRM with email marketing allows dealerships to segment their audience, personalize messaging, and track the effectiveness of campaigns. By analyzing data from CRM, dealerships can gain insights into customer behavior, preferences, and purchase history, enabling more targeted and effective email marketing strategies.

Conclusion

Digital marketing is a powerful tool for car dealerships to reach and engage potential customers. By implementing effective SEO strategies, creating valuable content, leveraging social media platforms, and utilizing email marketing, dealerships can build a strong online presence, attract high-quality leads, and drive sales. In the following chapters, we will explore advanced digital marketing techniques, including paid advertising, data analytics, and customer relationship management, to further enhance the dealership's marketing efforts.

Part 2: Integrating AI into Car Dealership Marketing
Chapter 5: Introduction to AI in Marketing

As the digital landscape evolves, the integration of artificial intelligence (AI) into marketing strategies has become increasingly important. AI is transforming how businesses operate, allowing them to gain deeper insights, automate processes, and enhance customer experiences. For car dealerships, leveraging AI can provide a significant competitive advantage, enabling them to better understand customer needs, optimize marketing efforts, and improve overall efficiency.

This chapter introduces the concept of AI, explores key AI technologies relevant to marketing, and discusses how car dealerships can begin incorporating AI into their marketing strategies.

What is AI?

Artificial Intelligence (AI) refers to the simulation of human intelligence in machines, enabling them to perform tasks that typically require human cognition. These tasks include learning, reasoning, problem-solving, perception, and natural language processing. AI systems use data to recognize patterns, make decisions, and improve over time, allowing them to perform complex tasks more efficiently and accurately than humans.

AI can be broadly categorized into three types:

> **Narrow AI (Weak AI)**: This type of AI is designed to perform specific tasks and is the most common form of AI in use today. Examples include virtual assistants (like Siri and Alexa), recommendation algorithms (used by Netflix and Amazon), and customer service chatbots.

General AI (Strong AI): General AI refers to machines that possess the ability to understand, learn, and apply knowledge across a wide range of tasks, similar to human intelligence. This type of AI remains theoretical and has not yet been achieved.

Superintelligent AI: This hypothetical form of AI would surpass human intelligence and capabilities across all fields. While the concept of superintelligent AI has sparked philosophical and ethical debates, it remains a topic of speculation and future research.

Key AI Technologies Relevant to Marketing

AI encompasses a variety of technologies that can be applied to marketing, each offering unique benefits and applications. Understanding these technologies is essential for car dealerships looking to integrate AI into their marketing strategies.

1. Machine Learning (ML)

Machine learning is a subset of AI that involves training algorithms to learn from data and make predictions or decisions without explicit programming. ML algorithms analyze large datasets, identify patterns, and improve their accuracy over time. In marketing, ML can be used for tasks such as customer segmentation, predictive analytics, and personalized recommendations.

- **Supervised Learning**: In this approach, the algorithm is trained on labeled data, meaning the input and output are provided. The algorithm learns to map inputs to the correct outputs. For example, supervised learning can be used to predict whether a customer is likely to buy a car based on their online behavior.

- **Unsupervised Learning**: Here, the algorithm is trained on unlabeled data and must identify patterns and relationships within the data on its own. Unsupervised learning is often used for customer segmentation, where the algorithm groups customers with similar behaviors or characteristics.

- **Reinforcement Learning**: This type of learning involves training an algorithm to make decisions by rewarding desired outcomes and penalizing undesired ones. Reinforcement learning can be used in dynamic pricing models, where the algorithm learns to adjust prices based on market conditions and customer responses.

2. Natural Language Processing (NLP)

Natural Language Processing (NLP) is a branch of AI that focuses on the interaction between computers and human language. NLP enables machines to understand, interpret, and generate human language, making it a valuable tool for customer communication and content creation.

- **Sentiment Analysis**: NLP can analyze customer reviews, social media posts, and feedback to determine the sentiment (positive, negative, or neutral). This helps dealerships understand customer opinions and improve their products and services.

- **Chatbots**: NLP-powered chatbots can engage with customers in real time, answer questions, provide product information, and assist with inquiries. Chatbots enhance customer service by providing instant responses and handling multiple interactions simultaneously.

- **Voice Recognition**: AI-driven voice recognition technology allows customers to interact with devices using voice commands. This can be applied in virtual assistants, voice search optimization, and customer support.

3. Computer Vision

Computer vision is an AI technology that enables machines to interpret and understand visual information from the world, such as images and videos. In marketing, computer vision can be used for visual search, product recognition, and augmented reality applications.

- **Visual Search**: Customers can upload images of vehicles they are interested in, and the AI system can identify similar models available at the dealership. This provides a seamless and interactive shopping experience.

- **Augmented Reality (AR)**: AR technology overlays digital information onto the real world, allowing customers to visualize vehicles in different colors, configurations, or environments. AR can enhance the online shopping experience and help customers make informed decisions.

4. Predictive Analytics

Predictive analytics involves using historical data, machine learning, and statistical algorithms to predict future outcomes. In marketing, predictive analytics can help dealerships anticipate customer behavior, optimize marketing campaigns, and improve sales forecasting.

- **Lead Scoring**: Predictive analytics can score leads based on their likelihood to convert, allowing sales teams to prioritize high-quality leads and improve conversion rates.

- **Customer Lifetime Value (CLV)**: By analyzing past customer data, predictive analytics can estimate the lifetime value of a customer, helping dealerships allocate marketing resources more effectively.

5. Personalization Engines

Personalization engines use AI to deliver personalized experiences to customers based on their preferences, behaviors, and past interactions. Personalization enhances customer engagement, improves satisfaction, and increases conversion rates.

- **Product Recommendations**: AI-driven recommendation engines can suggest vehicles, accessories, or services based on a customer's browsing history, purchase behavior, and preferences.

- **Customized Marketing Campaigns**: Personalization engines can tailor marketing messages, email content, and offers to individual customers, making them more relevant and compelling.

Benefits of AI in Car Dealership Marketing

Integrating AI into car dealership marketing offers numerous benefits that can drive business growth and improve customer experiences. Some key advantages include:

Enhanced Customer Insights

AI enables dealerships to gather and analyze vast amounts of customer data, providing valuable insights into customer preferences, behaviors, and needs. This data-driven approach allows dealerships to make informed decisions and tailor their marketing strategies to better meet customer expectations.

Improved Efficiency and Productivity

AI automates time-consuming tasks such as data analysis, lead scoring, and customer support, freeing up valuable time for marketing and sales teams. This increased efficiency allows teams to focus on high-value activities, such as building relationships and closing deals.

Personalized Customer Experiences

AI-powered personalization enhances the customer experience by delivering relevant and targeted content, recommendations, and offers. Personalization builds customer loyalty, improves engagement, and increases the likelihood of conversion.

Accurate Predictive Analytics

AI-driven predictive analytics allows dealerships to forecast market trends, customer behavior, and sales performance with greater accuracy. This predictive capability helps dealerships make proactive decisions, optimize inventory management, and plan effective marketing campaigns.

Scalability

AI solutions can scale to handle large volumes of data and interactions, making them suitable for dealerships of all sizes. As the business grows, AI can continue to provide valuable insights and support without the need for significant manual intervention.

Getting Started with AI in Marketing

For car dealerships looking to integrate AI into their marketing strategies, it's important to start with a clear plan and a focus on specific use cases that align with business goals. Here are some steps to get started:

Define Objectives

Identify the key marketing objectives that AI can help achieve, such as improving lead generation, enhancing customer service, or optimizing advertising spend. Defining clear objectives will guide the selection of AI tools and technologies.

Collect and Organize Data

Data is the foundation of AI. Ensure that the dealership has access to relevant and high-quality data, including customer information, sales data, website analytics, and social media interactions. Organize and store data in a centralized system to facilitate analysis and insights.

Choose the Right AI Tools

Evaluate AI tools and platforms that align with the dealership's needs and objectives. Consider factors such as ease of use, integration capabilities, scalability, and support. Starting with a few key tools, such as chatbots or predictive analytics software, can provide valuable experience and demonstrate the potential of AI.

Implement and Test

Implement AI solutions in a phased approach, starting with pilot projects to test and refine the technology. Monitor performance, gather feedback, and make adjustments as needed to optimize results.

Train and Educate Staff

Provide training and resources to help staff understand and utilize AI tools effectively. Encourage a culture of learning and experimentation, and involve employees in the process of integrating AI into the dealership's operations.

Measure and Optimize

Continuously measure the impact of AI on marketing performance using key performance indicators (KPIs) such as conversion rates, customer satisfaction, and return on investment (ROI). Use insights gained from AI to optimize marketing strategies and drive ongoing improvement.

Conclusion

AI is revolutionizing the marketing landscape, offering car dealerships powerful tools to enhance customer engagement, optimize operations, and drive growth. By understanding the key AI technologies relevant to marketing and taking a strategic approach to implementation, dealerships can harness the full potential of AI to gain a competitive edge. In the following chapters, we will explore specific AI applications in customer insights, advertising, lead generation, and more, providing a comprehensive guide to leveraging AI in car dealership marketing.

Chapter 6: AI-Driven Customer Insights

In the automotive industry, understanding customer needs, preferences, and behaviors is crucial for crafting effective marketing strategies and driving sales. AI-driven customer insights provide car dealerships with the ability to analyze vast amounts of data, uncover hidden patterns, and predict future behavior. By leveraging these insights, dealerships can deliver personalized experiences, improve customer satisfaction, and ultimately boost sales.

This chapter explores how AI can be used to collect and analyze customer data, the role of predictive analytics in marketing, and the ways in which personalization can enhance the customer experience.

Data Collection and Analysis

AI's ability to process and analyze large datasets quickly and accurately is one of its most powerful features. For car dealerships, collecting and analyzing customer data can provide valuable insights into buying habits, preferences, and behaviors. The key to leveraging AI for customer insights lies in effective data collection and analysis.

1. Sources of Customer Data

Customer data can be gathered from various sources, both online and offline, providing a comprehensive view of customer interactions and behaviors. Key data sources include:

- **Website Analytics**: Tracking customer interactions on the dealership's website, such as page views, click-through rates, time spent on site, and forms filled out, can reveal customer interests and intentions.

- **Social Media**: Analyzing customer engagement on social media platforms, including likes, shares, comments, and direct messages, helps dealerships understand customer sentiment and identify trends.

- **CRM Systems**: Customer Relationship Management (CRM) systems store valuable customer data, including contact information, purchase history, service records, and previous interactions with the dealership.

- **Sales and Service Data**: Data from sales transactions, service appointments, and customer feedback can provide insights into customer satisfaction, buying preferences, and maintenance needs.

- **Third-Party Data**: External data sources, such as market research reports, industry benchmarks, and demographic data, can complement internal data and provide additional context for analysis.

2. AI-Driven Data Analysis

Once data is collected, AI can be used to analyze and interpret it, uncovering patterns and generating actionable insights. AI-driven data analysis involves several key processes:

- **Data Cleansing and Integration**: AI tools can clean, organize, and integrate data from multiple sources, ensuring accuracy and consistency. This process helps eliminate duplicates, fill in missing information, and create a unified view of the customer.

- **Pattern Recognition**: Machine learning algorithms can identify patterns and trends in customer behavior, such as common purchase paths, preferred vehicle features, or seasonal buying trends. Recognizing these patterns enables dealerships to tailor their marketing strategies and offerings.

- **Customer Segmentation**: AI can segment customers into groups based on shared characteristics, such as demographics, buying behavior, or interests. Customer segmentation allows dealerships to target specific audiences with personalized messages and offers.

- **Sentiment Analysis**: Using natural language processing (NLP), AI can analyze customer reviews, social media posts, and feedback to gauge sentiment and identify positive or negative opinions. Sentiment analysis helps dealerships address customer concerns and improve their products and services.

Predictive Analytics and Personalization

Predictive analytics uses historical data, machine learning, and statistical models to predict future outcomes. In car dealership marketing, predictive analytics can forecast customer behavior, sales trends, and marketing campaign performance. Personalization, on the other hand, involves tailoring the customer experience to individual preferences and needs, making interactions more relevant and engaging.

1. **Predictive Analytics Applications**
    - **Lead Scoring and Prioritization**: Predictive analytics can score leads based on their likelihood to convert, allowing sales teams to focus on high-quality leads. By analyzing factors such as online behavior, past interactions, and demographic data, AI can predict which leads are most likely to make a purchase.

    - **Sales Forecasting**: AI can analyze historical sales data and market trends to forecast future sales performance. Accurate sales forecasting helps dealerships manage inventory, plan marketing campaigns, and set realistic sales targets.

- **Churn Prediction**: Predictive analytics can identify customers at risk of leaving or becoming inactive. By analyzing customer behavior, purchase history, and engagement levels, AI can predict churn and enable dealerships to take proactive measures to retain customers.

- **Demand Forecasting**: Predictive analytics can forecast demand for specific vehicle models, features, or services. By understanding customer preferences and market trends, dealerships can optimize inventory and reduce the risk of overstocking or understocking.

2. Personalization Strategies

- **Personalized Recommendations**: AI-driven recommendation engines can suggest vehicles, accessories, or services based on a customer's browsing history, purchase behavior, and preferences. Personalized recommendations increase the likelihood of conversion and enhance the shopping experience.

- **Targeted Marketing Campaigns**: AI can analyze customer data to create targeted marketing campaigns that resonate with specific audience segments. By delivering personalized messages, offers, and content, dealerships can improve engagement and drive sales.

- **Dynamic Content Personalization**: AI can dynamically change website content, email messages, and advertisements based on the customer's behavior and preferences. For example, a returning customer may see tailored promotions or personalized greetings when visiting the dealership's website.

- **Predictive Maintenance Offers**: Using data from connected vehicles and service records, AI can predict when a customer's vehicle may need maintenance or repairs. Dealerships can send personalized maintenance reminders, offers, or service recommendations to encourage customers to visit the service department.

Enhancing Customer Experience with AI-Driven Insights

AI-driven customer insights not only help dealerships improve marketing strategies but also enhance the overall customer experience. By understanding customer needs and preferences, dealerships can provide a more personalized, efficient, and satisfying experience.

1. Improving Customer Engagement

AI enables dealerships to engage with customers more effectively by delivering relevant and timely content. Whether through personalized emails, targeted social media ads, or tailored website experiences, AI-driven insights ensure that customers receive information that matters to them. This targeted approach increases engagement, builds brand loyalty, and encourages repeat business.

2. Streamlining the Sales Process

AI-driven insights can streamline the sales process by providing sales teams with valuable information about customer preferences, buying behavior, and readiness to purchase. Sales representatives can use this information to tailor their approach, address customer concerns, and close deals more efficiently. Additionally, AI-powered chatbots can handle routine inquiries, freeing up sales staff to focus on high-value interactions.

3. Enhancing Customer Support

AI-driven insights can improve customer support by providing a better understanding of common issues, frequently asked questions, and customer sentiment. Chatbots equipped with AI and natural language processing can handle routine support requests, provide instant answers, and escalate complex issues to human agents. This ensures that customers receive timely and accurate support, improving satisfaction and loyalty.

4. Building Long-Term Relationships

By using AI to understand and anticipate customer needs, dealerships can build long-term relationships with their customers. Personalized communication, targeted offers, and proactive support demonstrate that the dealership values its customers and is committed to meeting their needs. Building strong relationships not only increases customer retention but also encourages positive word-of-mouth and referrals.

Conclusion

AI-driven customer insights offer car dealerships a powerful tool for understanding and engaging with their customers. By leveraging AI to collect, analyze, and interpret data, dealerships can gain valuable insights into customer behavior, predict future trends, and deliver personalized experiences. These insights enable dealerships to optimize marketing strategies, improve customer satisfaction, and drive business growth. In the following chapters, we will explore specific AI applications in areas such as advertising, lead generation, and customer support, providing a comprehensive guide to harnessing AI for car dealership marketing.

Chapter 7: Chatbots and Virtual Assistants

In an increasingly digital world, customers expect fast, efficient, and personalized service. Chatbots and virtual assistants have emerged as powerful tools to meet these expectations, offering immediate responses and personalized interactions. For car dealerships, implementing these AI-driven solutions can enhance customer engagement, streamline communication, and improve overall customer satisfaction.

This chapter delves into the role of chatbots and virtual assistants in automotive marketing, exploring their benefits, use cases, and best practices for implementation.

Enhancing Customer Interaction

Chatbots and virtual assistants use artificial intelligence to simulate human conversation, providing customers with real-time responses and assistance. They can handle a wide range of tasks, from answering simple queries to guiding customers through the car-buying process. By automating customer interactions, chatbots free up sales and support teams to focus on more complex issues, improving efficiency and customer experience.

1. **Benefits of Chatbots and Virtual Assistants**
   - **24/7 Availability**: Unlike human agents, chatbots are available around the clock, providing instant responses to customer inquiries at any time. This ensures that customers receive assistance even outside of business hours, improving accessibility and convenience.

   - **Immediate Response**: Chatbots can handle multiple interactions simultaneously, reducing wait times and providing immediate responses to customer queries. This quick response time enhances customer satisfaction and prevents potential customers from leaving the website due to delays.

- **Cost Efficiency**: By automating routine tasks and inquiries, chatbots can significantly reduce operational costs. They minimize the need for large customer support teams and can handle a high volume of interactions without additional resources.

- **Consistency**: Chatbots provide consistent and accurate information, ensuring that all customers receive the same level of service. This consistency helps build trust and reliability, essential components of a positive customer experience.

- **Data Collection and Insights**: Chatbots can collect valuable data on customer preferences, behaviors, and pain points. This data can be analyzed to gain insights into customer needs and improve marketing strategies.

2. Common Use Cases for Chatbots in Car Dealerships
    - **Answering Frequently Asked Questions (FAQs)**: Chatbots can quickly answer common questions about vehicle models, pricing, financing options, and dealership services. By handling these routine inquiries, chatbots free up human agents to focus on more complex customer needs.

    - **Lead Generation and Qualification**: Chatbots can engage with website visitors, ask qualifying questions, and gather contact information. This helps identify potential leads and qualify them based on their interests and readiness to buy. Qualified leads can then be passed on to the sales team for follow-up.

    - **Appointment Scheduling**: Chatbots can assist customers in scheduling test drives, service appointments, or consultations with sales representatives. By automating the appointment scheduling process, chatbots improve efficiency and reduce the likelihood of missed appointments.

- **Vehicle Recommendations**: Chatbots can guide customers through the car selection process by asking questions about their preferences, needs, and budget. Based on the responses, the chatbot can suggest suitable vehicle models and features, providing a personalized shopping experience.

- **Post-Purchase Support**: After a purchase, chatbots can assist customers with questions about vehicle maintenance, warranty coverage, or service scheduling. Providing ongoing support helps build long-term relationships and enhances customer loyalty.

3. Implementing Effective Chatbots

Implementing chatbots effectively requires careful planning and consideration of customer needs. Here are some best practices for successful chatbot implementation:

- **Define Objectives**: Clearly define the objectives of the chatbot, such as improving customer support, increasing lead generation, or enhancing customer engagement. Having clear goals will guide the development and deployment of the chatbot.

- **Choose the Right Platform**: Select a chatbot platform that aligns with the dealership's needs and capabilities. Consider factors such as ease of integration, customization options, scalability, and support. Platforms like Drift, Intercom, and Zendesk offer robust chatbot solutions tailored for businesses.

- **Design a User-Friendly Interface**: Ensure that the chatbot interface is intuitive and easy to use. Use clear and simple language, provide quick response options, and allow customers to easily navigate through the conversation. A user-friendly interface enhances the customer experience and encourages engagement.

- **Train the Chatbot**: Use machine learning and natural language processing (NLP) to train the chatbot to understand and respond to customer inquiries accurately. Continuously update and improve the chatbot's knowledge base to ensure it provides relevant and up-to-date information.

- **Provide Escalation Options**: While chatbots can handle many tasks, they should have the ability to escalate complex issues to human agents when necessary. Providing escalation options ensures that customers receive the appropriate level of support and prevents frustration.

- **Monitor and Optimize Performance**: Regularly monitor the chatbot's performance using metrics such as response time, customer satisfaction, and conversion rates. Gather feedback from customers to identify areas for improvement and optimize the chatbot's functionality.

Automating Customer Support

Customer support is a critical aspect of the car-buying process, and chatbots can play a significant role in automating and improving support services. By handling routine inquiries and providing quick assistance, chatbots enhance the customer experience and reduce the burden on support teams.

1. Handling Inquiries and Providing Information

Chatbots can handle a wide range of customer inquiries, including questions about vehicle specifications, pricing, financing options, and service availability. By providing accurate and timely information, chatbots help customers make informed decisions and move forward in their buying journey.

2. Assisting with Troubleshooting

For customers experiencing issues with their vehicles, chatbots can provide troubleshooting assistance. By asking diagnostic questions and offering solutions, chatbots can help customers resolve common problems or guide them to schedule a service appointment if necessary.

3. Supporting After-Sales Service

After a vehicle purchase, customers may have questions about maintenance, warranties, or service schedules. Chatbots can provide information about recommended maintenance intervals, warranty coverage, and available service packages. They can also assist with scheduling service appointments, ensuring that customers receive timely and convenient support.

4. Collecting Feedback and Reviews

Chatbots can be used to collect customer feedback and reviews, providing valuable insights into customer satisfaction and areas for improvement. By asking customers about their experience with the dealership, chatbots can gather feedback on sales interactions, service quality, and overall satisfaction. This feedback can be used to enhance customer service and improve business operations.

Conclusion

Chatbots and virtual assistants are transforming customer interactions in the automotive industry, offering a seamless and efficient way to engage with customers. By providing instant responses, personalized recommendations, and automated support, chatbots enhance the customer experience and drive business growth. For car dealerships, implementing chatbots and virtual assistants can improve customer satisfaction, streamline operations, and increase sales. In the next chapter, we will explore how AI can be used in advertising and lead generation, further enhancing the marketing capabilities of car dealerships.

Chapter 8: AI in Advertising and Lead Generation

Advertising and lead generation are critical components of a car dealership's marketing strategy. These efforts directly impact a dealership's ability to attract potential buyers, nurture leads, and convert them into loyal customers. Artificial intelligence (AI) offers powerful tools to enhance advertising effectiveness and optimize lead generation, allowing dealerships to reach the right audience with the right message at the right time.

This chapter will explore how AI can revolutionize advertising and lead generation for car dealerships, focusing on programmatic advertising, AI-powered lead scoring, and management techniques.

Programmatic Advertising

Programmatic advertising is an automated approach to buying and optimizing digital ad placements in real-time using AI and machine learning. Unlike traditional advertising methods, which rely on manual processes and negotiations, programmatic advertising allows dealerships to reach their target audience more efficiently and effectively.

1. What is Programmatic Advertising?

Programmatic advertising automates the buying, placement, and optimization of ad space using AI algorithms. It leverages data to make real-time decisions about which ads to show, to whom, and where. This process is typically done through demand-side platforms (DSPs) and supply-side platforms (SSPs), which facilitate the automated buying and selling of ad inventory.

2. Benefits of Programmatic Advertising for Car Dealerships
- **Precision Targeting**: Programmatic advertising allows dealerships to target specific audience segments based on

various factors, such as demographics, interests, browsing behavior, and location. This precision targeting ensures that ads reach the most relevant audience, increasing the likelihood of engagement and conversion.

- **Real-Time Optimization**: AI algorithms continuously analyze ad performance data and adjust campaigns in real-time to maximize effectiveness. This real-time optimization allows dealerships to allocate their budget more efficiently, focusing on ads that deliver the best results.

- **Cost Efficiency**: By automating the ad-buying process, programmatic advertising reduces the cost of manual negotiations and human error. It also enables dealerships to bid on ad inventory based on its value, ensuring cost-effective spending.

- **Scalability**: Programmatic advertising can scale campaigns quickly, reaching a large audience across multiple platforms and devices. This scalability is essential for dealerships looking to expand their reach and attract more potential customers.

3. Implementing Programmatic Advertising

To implement programmatic advertising effectively, car dealerships should follow these steps:

- **Define Campaign Goals**: Clearly define the objectives of the advertising campaign, such as brand awareness, lead generation, or vehicle sales. Having specific goals will guide the targeting and optimization strategies.

- **Choose the Right Platforms**: Select demand-side platforms (DSPs) that align with the dealership's goals and target audience. Popular DSPs include Google Ads, The Trade Desk, and MediaMath, each offering different features and capabilities.

- **Segment the Audience**: Use data to segment the target audience based on demographics, interests, behaviors, and other relevant factors. Audience segmentation allows for more personalized and relevant ad targeting.

- **Create Engaging Ad Content**: Develop compelling ad creatives that resonate with the target audience. Use high-quality images, videos, and persuasive messaging to capture attention and drive engagement.

- **Monitor and Optimize**: Continuously monitor ad performance using key performance indicators (KPIs) such as click-through rates (CTR), conversion rates, and return on ad spend (ROAS). Use AI-driven insights to optimize campaigns in real-time, adjusting bids, targeting, and creatives as needed.

AI-Powered Lead Scoring and Management

Lead generation is a crucial aspect of car dealership marketing, and AI can significantly enhance the efficiency and effectiveness of lead scoring and management processes. By analyzing data and predicting lead behavior, AI helps dealerships prioritize high-quality leads, allocate resources more effectively, and improve conversion rates.

1. What is Lead Scoring?

Lead scoring is the process of assigning a value or score to each lead based on their likelihood to convert into a customer. This score is determined by analyzing various factors, such as the lead's behavior, engagement level, demographics, and interactions with the dealership. High-scoring leads are prioritized for follow-up by the sales team, increasing the chances of conversion.

2. How AI Enhances Lead Scoring

AI-powered lead scoring goes beyond traditional methods by leveraging machine learning algorithms to analyze large datasets and identify patterns that indicate a lead's likelihood to convert. AI can evaluate factors such as:

- **Website Behavior**: AI analyzes a lead's interactions with the dealership's website, including pages visited, time spent on site, and actions taken (e.g., downloading a brochure or scheduling a test drive).

- **Engagement with Marketing Campaigns**: AI tracks a lead's engagement with email campaigns, social media ads, and other marketing efforts, assessing their level of interest and responsiveness.

- **Demographic Data**: AI considers demographic information, such as age, location, and income level, to determine the lead's suitability for specific vehicle models or offers.

- **Past Purchase History**: For returning customers, AI analyzes past purchase behavior and service records to predict future buying intent and preferences.

3. Implementing AI-Powered Lead Scoring

To implement AI-powered lead scoring, car dealerships should:

- **Integrate Data Sources**: Collect data from various sources, such as website analytics, CRM systems, email marketing platforms, and social media channels. Integrating these data sources provides a comprehensive view of each lead.

- **Define Scoring Criteria**: Determine the factors that contribute to a lead's likelihood to convert, such as website behavior, engagement levels, and demographic information. Assign weights to each factor based on its importance.

- **Use AI Tools**: Utilize AI-powered lead scoring tools, such as HubSpot, Marketo, or Salesforce Einstein, to automate the scoring process. These tools use machine learning algorithms to analyze data and assign scores to leads in real-time.

- **Prioritize Leads**: Use the lead scores to prioritize follow-up efforts. High-scoring leads should be contacted promptly by the sales team, while low-scoring leads can be nurtured through targeted marketing campaigns.

- **Continuously Improve**: Regularly review and refine the lead scoring model based on feedback and performance data. Adjust the scoring criteria and weights to improve accuracy and effectiveness.

AI in Lead Management

In addition to lead scoring, AI can streamline lead management processes, ensuring that leads are nurtured effectively and moved through the sales funnel efficiently. AI-driven lead management tools automate tasks, personalize communication, and provide valuable insights into lead behavior.

1. Automating Lead Nurturing

AI can automate lead nurturing by sending personalized emails, messages, and content based on a lead's behavior and preferences. For example, if a lead shows interest in a specific vehicle model, AI can send targeted content about that model, including features, reviews, and special offers. Automated lead nurturing keeps leads engaged and informed, increasing the likelihood of conversion.

2. Predicting Lead Behavior

AI can predict a lead's behavior and readiness to buy by analyzing data from multiple touchpoints. For instance, AI can identify when a lead is nearing the decision stage based on their interactions with the dealership's website, emails, and sales team. Predicting lead behavior enables sales representatives to time their follow-ups effectively, maximizing the chances of closing the deal.

3. Personalizing Communication

Personalization is key to effective lead management. AI can tailor communication based on a lead's preferences, interests, and past interactions. Personalized messages resonate more with leads, making them feel valued and understood. This personalized approach enhances the customer experience and builds trust, increasing the likelihood of conversion.

4. Analyzing Lead Data

AI can analyze lead data to provide insights into lead quality, campaign effectiveness, and sales performance. By understanding which sources and campaigns generate the highest-quality leads, dealerships can optimize their marketing efforts and allocate resources more effectively. Data-driven insights help improve lead generation strategies and drive better results.

Conclusion

AI is transforming advertising and lead generation for car dealerships, offering powerful tools to reach, engage, and convert potential customers. Programmatic advertising enables precision targeting and real-time optimization, ensuring that marketing efforts are efficient and effective. AI-powered lead scoring and management streamline the lead generation process, prioritizing high-quality leads and personalizing communication to enhance the customer experience. By leveraging AI in advertising and lead generation, car dealerships can drive better results, improve customer satisfaction, and grow their business.

In the next part of the book, we will explore advanced AI applications in pricing, inventory management, and after-sales services, further enhancing the capabilities of car dealerships in the digital age.

Part 3: Advanced AI Applications in Dealerships

Chapter 9: AI in Pricing and Inventory Management

Effective pricing and inventory management are crucial for maximizing profitability and meeting customer demand in the automotive industry. Artificial intelligence (AI) offers advanced tools to optimize pricing strategies and manage inventory more efficiently, helping car dealerships make data-driven decisions and stay competitive in a dynamic market.

This chapter explores how AI can be utilized in pricing and inventory management, focusing on dynamic pricing models, inventory optimization, and best practices for implementation.

Dynamic Pricing Models

Dynamic pricing is a pricing strategy where the price of a product or service is adjusted in real-time based on various factors such as demand, competition, and market conditions. AI-powered dynamic pricing models enable car dealerships to optimize their pricing strategies and respond quickly to market changes.

1. What is Dynamic Pricing?

Dynamic pricing involves using algorithms to adjust prices based on real-time data and market conditions. Unlike static pricing, which remains fixed over time, dynamic pricing allows dealerships to vary prices to maximize revenue, manage inventory, and remain competitive.

2. Benefits of AI-Powered Dynamic Pricing
- **Maximizes Revenue**: By adjusting prices based on demand and market conditions, dynamic pricing helps dealerships capture the

highest possible revenue for each vehicle. AI algorithms analyze data to set optimal prices that balance demand and profitability.

- **Improves Competitiveness**: AI-powered dynamic pricing enables dealerships to stay competitive by adjusting prices in response to competitors' pricing strategies. This ensures that the dealership remains attractive to potential buyers while maintaining profitability.

- **Optimizes Inventory Management**: Dynamic pricing can help manage inventory levels by adjusting prices based on vehicle availability and demand. For example, if a particular model is overstocked, the pricing algorithm can lower the price to accelerate sales and reduce inventory levels.

- **Enhances Customer Experience**: AI-powered dynamic pricing can offer personalized pricing based on customer preferences and behavior. This personalized approach improves the customer experience and increases the likelihood of conversion.

3. Implementing Dynamic Pricing

To implement AI-powered dynamic pricing, car dealerships should follow these steps:

- **Collect Data**: Gather data on vehicle sales, market conditions, competitor prices, and customer behavior. This data provides the foundation for dynamic pricing algorithms and helps identify pricing patterns and trends.

- **Choose a Pricing Platform**: Select a dynamic pricing platform that integrates with the dealership's existing systems and offers real-time pricing adjustments. Platforms such as Pricefx, PROS, and Zilliant provide advanced dynamic pricing solutions.

- **Define Pricing Rules**: Establish pricing rules and parameters based on factors such as demand, inventory levels, and competitor pricing. Define thresholds for price adjustments to ensure that pricing remains competitive and profitable.

- **Monitor and Optimize**: Continuously monitor the performance of the dynamic pricing model and make adjustments as needed. Analyze key performance indicators (KPIs) such as sales volume, revenue, and profit margins to assess the effectiveness of the pricing strategy.

- **Communicate Changes**: Clearly communicate pricing changes to customers to maintain transparency and trust. Use marketing channels such as email, social media, and website notifications to inform customers of promotions and special offers.

Inventory Optimization

Effective inventory management is essential for ensuring that the right vehicles are available to meet customer demand while minimizing excess inventory. AI-powered inventory optimization tools help dealerships manage their inventory more efficiently, reduce costs, and improve profitability.

1. What is Inventory Optimization?

Inventory optimization involves using AI and machine learning algorithms to manage inventory levels and ensure that the right mix of vehicles is available at the right time. This process aims to balance supply and demand, minimize carrying costs, and maximize sales.

2. Benefits of AI-Powered Inventory Optimization
- **Reduces Carrying Costs**: AI-powered inventory optimization helps dealerships minimize carrying costs by predicting demand and adjusting inventory levels accordingly. This reduces the costs

associated with holding excess inventory and frees up capital for other investments.

- **Improves Demand Forecasting**: AI algorithms analyze historical sales data, market trends, and external factors to forecast future demand accurately. This helps dealerships plan inventory levels more effectively and avoid stockouts or overstock situations.

- **Enhances Inventory Turnover**: By optimizing inventory levels, AI-powered tools improve inventory turnover rates, ensuring that vehicles are sold within an optimal timeframe. This reduces the risk of vehicles becoming obsolete and losing value.

- **Optimizes Pricing and Promotions**: AI can analyze inventory data to identify opportunities for pricing adjustments and promotions. For example, if a particular model is slow-moving, AI can recommend discounts or special offers to boost sales and reduce inventory.

3. Implementing AI-Powered Inventory Optimization

To implement AI-powered inventory optimization, car dealerships should:

- **Integrate Data Sources**: Collect data from various sources, such as sales records, inventory levels, and market trends. Integrating these data sources provides a comprehensive view of inventory performance and demand patterns.

- **Select an Optimization Platform**: Choose an inventory optimization platform that offers advanced analytics and forecasting capabilities. Platforms such as Cloudera, IBM Watson, and Oracle provide AI-driven inventory management solutions.

- **Set Inventory Parameters**: Define parameters for inventory optimization, such as minimum and maximum stock levels, reorder points, and lead times. These parameters help guide inventory decisions and ensure that the right vehicles are available at the right time.

- **Monitor and Adjust**: Continuously monitor inventory performance and make adjustments as needed. Analyze KPIs such as inventory turnover, carrying costs, and sales performance to assess the effectiveness of the inventory optimization strategy.

- **Collaborate with Suppliers**: Work closely with vehicle manufacturers and suppliers to ensure a steady supply of vehicles and address any supply chain issues. Effective collaboration helps maintain inventory levels and avoid disruptions.

Conclusion

AI is revolutionizing pricing and inventory management in the automotive industry, offering advanced tools to optimize pricing strategies and manage inventory more efficiently. Dynamic pricing models enable dealerships to adjust prices in real-time based on market conditions and demand, maximizing revenue and competitiveness. AI-powered inventory optimization tools help manage inventory levels, reduce carrying costs, and improve profitability. By leveraging AI in pricing and inventory management, car dealerships can enhance their operational efficiency, meet customer demand, and drive business growth.

In the next chapter, we will explore how AI can enhance the customer experience, including virtual showrooms, test drives, and personalized interactions.

Chapter 10: Enhancing the Customer Experience with AI

In the competitive automotive market, providing an exceptional customer experience is key to attracting and retaining buyers. Artificial intelligence (AI) can significantly enhance the customer experience by offering personalized interactions, streamlining processes, and creating immersive experiences. This chapter explores how AI can transform the customer experience in car dealerships, focusing on virtual showrooms, test drives, and AI-enhanced personalization.

Virtual Showrooms and Test Drives

Virtual showrooms and test drives offer a cutting-edge way for customers to explore vehicles and engage with the dealership from the comfort of their own homes. AI-powered technologies make these experiences more immersive and interactive, providing potential buyers with a comprehensive view of the vehicles and their features.

1. What are Virtual Showrooms?

Virtual showrooms are digital environments where customers can browse and interact with vehicle models using their computers or mobile devices. These showrooms offer a realistic and engaging experience, allowing customers to view vehicles from different angles, explore interior features, and even customize their options.

2. Benefits of Virtual Showrooms

- **Enhanced Accessibility**: Virtual showrooms allow customers to explore vehicle options at their convenience, without the need to visit the dealership in person. This accessibility can attract a wider audience and cater to customers who may not be able to visit the physical location.

- **Increased Engagement**: Interactive virtual showrooms provide an engaging experience by allowing customers to customize vehicles, view different color options, and explore features in detail. This increased engagement can lead to higher interest and conversion rates.

- **Cost Efficiency**: Virtual showrooms reduce the need for physical inventory and showroom space, leading to cost savings for the dealership. They also enable dealerships to showcase a broader range of vehicles without the constraints of physical space.

- **Data Collection**: Virtual showrooms collect valuable data on customer interactions and preferences. This data can be used to personalize marketing efforts, follow up with leads, and improve the overall customer experience.

3. Implementing Virtual Showrooms

To implement a virtual showroom, car dealerships should:

- **Choose a Platform**: Select a virtual showroom platform that offers high-quality 3D visuals, interactive features, and integration with the dealership's existing systems. Platforms such as Matterport, 3DClouds, and Vroom provide advanced virtual showroom solutions.

- **Create High-Quality Content**: Develop realistic 3D models of vehicles, including detailed interior and exterior views. Use high-resolution images and videos to enhance the visual appeal and accuracy of the virtual showroom.

- **Integrate Customization Options**: Allow customers to customize vehicles by selecting colors, trims, and features. Provide real-time updates to show how changes affect the vehicle's appearance and specifications.

- **Promote the Virtual Showroom**: Market the virtual showroom through the dealership's website, social media channels, and email campaigns. Highlight the convenience and benefits of the virtual experience to attract potential buyers.

- **Analyze Performance**: Monitor customer interactions and engagement with the virtual showroom. Use data to assess the effectiveness of the virtual showroom and make improvements based on customer feedback and behavior.

4. Virtual Test Drives

Virtual test drives use AI and simulation technologies to provide customers with an immersive driving experience. These simulations allow customers to experience the vehicle's performance, handling, and features without leaving their homes.

Benefits of Virtual Test Drives

- **Realistic Experience**: Virtual test drives offer a realistic simulation of the vehicle's performance, allowing customers to experience driving conditions, acceleration, and handling.

- **Convenience**: Customers can take virtual test drives at their convenience, eliminating the need for scheduling and visiting the dealership. This convenience can lead to increased interest and engagement.

- **Safe and Inclusive**: Virtual test drives provide a safe way for customers to explore vehicles without physical risk. They also cater to customers who may have mobility issues or other barriers to visiting the dealership.

- **Enhanced Marketing**: Virtual test drives can be used as part of marketing campaigns to attract potential buyers. They offer a unique and engaging way to showcase a vehicle's features and performance.

AI-Enhanced Personalization

AI-powered personalization enhances the customer experience by tailoring interactions, recommendations, and offers based on individual preferences and behaviors. Personalization can significantly improve customer satisfaction and increase the likelihood of conversion.

1. Personalized Recommendations

AI algorithms analyze customer data to provide personalized vehicle recommendations based on factors such as browsing history, previous interactions, and purchase behavior. By offering relevant recommendations, dealerships can improve the customer experience and increase the chances of finding the perfect vehicle.

Benefits of Personalized Recommendations

- **Increased Relevance**: Personalized recommendations ensure that customers receive information and offers that are relevant to their interests and preferences. This relevance enhances the customer experience and reduces frustration.

- **Higher Engagement**: Customers are more likely to engage with content and offers that are tailored to their needs. Personalized recommendations can lead to higher click-through rates and conversion rates.

- **Improved Customer Satisfaction**: By providing recommendations that align with customer preferences, dealerships can enhance overall satisfaction and build stronger relationships with customers.

2. AI-Driven Customer Service

AI-driven customer service tools, such as chatbots and virtual assistants, provide personalized support and assistance to customers. These tools use natural language processing (NLP) and machine learning to understand and respond to customer inquiries effectively.

Benefits of AI-Driven Customer Service

- **24/7 Availability**: AI-driven customer service tools are available around the clock, providing instant support and assistance to customers at any time. This availability improves customer satisfaction and ensures timely responses.

- **Efficient Handling of Inquiries**: AI tools can handle a large volume of inquiries simultaneously, reducing wait times and improving efficiency. They can provide accurate and consistent answers to common questions, freeing up human agents for more complex tasks.

- **Personalized Assistance**: AI-driven customer service tools can personalize interactions based on customer data and previous interactions. This personalization enhances the customer experience and provides relevant support.

- **Data Insights**: AI tools collect and analyze data on customer interactions, providing valuable insights into customer needs and preferences. This data can be used to improve service quality and identify areas for improvement.

3. Tailored Marketing Campaigns

AI can optimize marketing campaigns by analyzing customer data and segmenting audiences based on their preferences and behaviors. Tailored marketing campaigns target specific segments with personalized messages and offers, increasing the effectiveness of marketing efforts.

Benefits of Tailored Marketing Campaigns

- **Higher Conversion Rates**: Targeted campaigns are more likely to resonate with customers, leading to higher conversion rates. Personalized offers and messages are more relevant and engaging.

- **Improved ROI**: By focusing on high-value segments and delivering relevant content, tailored marketing campaigns can improve return on investment (ROI) and reduce wasted ad spend.

- **Enhanced Customer Experience**: Personalized marketing campaigns create a more relevant and enjoyable experience for customers, leading to increased satisfaction and loyalty.

Conclusion

AI is transforming the customer experience in car dealerships by offering innovative solutions such as virtual showrooms, test drives, and personalized interactions. These technologies enhance accessibility, engagement, and convenience, providing customers with a more immersive and tailored experience. By leveraging AI to improve the customer experience, car dealerships can attract and retain buyers, increase satisfaction, and drive business growth.

In the next chapter, we will explore how AI can be applied to after-sales services, including predictive maintenance, upselling, and customer retention strategies.

Chapter 11: AI in After-Sales Services

After-sales services are crucial for maintaining customer satisfaction, fostering loyalty, and driving repeat business. Artificial intelligence (AI) plays a significant role in enhancing after-sales services by providing predictive maintenance, upselling opportunities, and effective customer retention strategies. This chapter explores how AI can be utilized to optimize after-sales services in car dealerships, focusing on predictive maintenance, upselling, and customer retention.

Predictive Maintenance and Upselling

Predictive maintenance and upselling are essential components of after-sales services that ensure vehicle reliability, maximize revenue, and enhance the overall customer experience. AI technologies enable dealerships to offer more proactive and personalized maintenance services while identifying opportunities for additional sales.

1. What is Predictive Maintenance?

Predictive maintenance involves using AI and machine learning algorithms to predict when a vehicle will require maintenance or repairs based on data from various sources. This proactive approach helps prevent breakdowns, reduce repair costs, and improve vehicle reliability.

2. Benefits of Predictive Maintenance
- **Reduced Downtime**: Predictive maintenance helps identify potential issues before they lead to breakdowns, minimizing vehicle downtime and keeping customers satisfied.

- **Cost Savings**: By addressing maintenance issues early, dealerships can reduce the need for costly emergency repairs and extend the lifespan of vehicle components.

- **Enhanced Customer Satisfaction**: Proactive maintenance services show customers that the dealership is committed to their vehicle's performance and longevity, leading to higher satisfaction and loyalty.

- **Optimized Service Scheduling**: AI algorithms can optimize service scheduling based on predicted maintenance needs, ensuring that service appointments are well-timed and efficiently managed.

3. Implementing Predictive Maintenance

To implement predictive maintenance, car dealerships should:

- **Collect Data**: Gather data from vehicle sensors, telematics systems, and historical service records. This data provides insights into vehicle performance and maintenance needs.

- **Use AI Algorithms**: Apply AI and machine learning algorithms to analyze data and predict maintenance needs. Platforms such as Bosch Automotive, Uptake, and Pivotal offer predictive maintenance solutions.

- **Monitor Vehicle Health**: Continuously monitor vehicle health data to identify potential issues and schedule maintenance appointments as needed.

- **Communicate with Customers**: Inform customers about upcoming maintenance needs and provide recommendations for service. Use automated notifications and reminders to keep customers informed and engaged.

- **Analyze Performance**: Evaluate the effectiveness of predictive maintenance by tracking key performance indicators (KPIs) such as service frequency, repair costs, and customer satisfaction.

4. AI-Driven Upselling Opportunities

AI can also identify opportunities for upselling additional services and products based on customer data and vehicle condition. By analyzing customer behavior and vehicle usage patterns, AI can recommend relevant products and services that enhance the vehicle's performance and value.

Benefits of AI-Driven Upselling

- **Increased Revenue**: AI-driven upselling helps dealerships increase revenue by recommending additional services, such as extended warranties, premium maintenance packages, or accessory upgrades.

- **Personalized Recommendations**: AI algorithms provide personalized recommendations based on the customer's vehicle history and preferences, improving the relevance of upsell offers.

- **Enhanced Customer Experience**: By offering relevant and timely upsell opportunities, dealerships can enhance the customer experience and build stronger relationships with their clients.

Implementing AI-Driven Upselling

To implement AI-driven upselling, dealerships should:

- **Analyze Customer Data**: Use AI to analyze customer data, including service history, vehicle usage, and purchase patterns. This analysis helps identify opportunities for upselling.

- **Integrate Upsell Recommendations**: Incorporate AI-generated upsell recommendations into service interactions, such as during maintenance appointments or through digital communication channels.

- **Monitor Performance**: Track the effectiveness of upsell campaigns by measuring conversion rates, revenue generated, and customer feedback. Use this data to refine upselling strategies and improve results.

Customer Retention Strategies

Customer retention is a critical aspect of after-sales services, as retaining existing customers is often more cost-effective than acquiring new ones. AI can enhance customer retention by providing personalized experiences, improving communication, and addressing customer needs more effectively.

1. Personalized Communication

AI can personalize communication with customers by analyzing their preferences, service history, and interactions with the dealership. Personalized communication ensures that customers receive relevant information and offers, enhancing their overall experience.

Benefits of Personalized Communication

- **Increased Engagement**: Personalized messages are more likely to resonate with customers and encourage engagement. This leads to higher response rates and customer interaction.

- **Improved Customer Loyalty**: By addressing customers by name and tailoring communication to their preferences, dealerships can build stronger relationships and foster loyalty.

- **Enhanced Service Experience**: Personalized communication ensures that customers receive timely and relevant information about their vehicles, service appointments, and special offers.

Implementing Personalized Communication

To implement personalized communication, dealerships should:

- **Segment Customer Data**: Use AI to segment customer data based on factors such as service history, preferences, and demographics. This segmentation helps tailor communication to different customer groups.

- **Automate Communication**: Implement AI-driven tools to automate communication processes, such as sending personalized emails, notifications, and reminders.

- **Track Engagement**: Monitor customer engagement with personalized communication and adjust strategies based on response rates and feedback.

2. AI-Driven Customer Feedback and Support

AI tools can analyze customer feedback and support interactions to identify trends, address issues, and improve service quality. By leveraging AI to analyze feedback, dealerships can proactively address customer concerns and enhance their overall service experience.

Benefits of AI-Driven Customer Feedback and Support

- **Faster Issue Resolution**: AI tools can quickly identify and address common customer issues, leading to faster resolution and improved satisfaction.

- **Actionable Insights**: Analyzing customer feedback provides valuable insights into areas for improvement and helps dealerships make data-driven decisions to enhance their services.

- **Proactive Support**: AI can predict potential customer issues based on feedback and interactions, allowing dealerships to address concerns before they escalate.

Implementing AI-Driven Customer Feedback and Support

To implement AI-driven customer feedback and support, dealerships should:

- **Collect and Analyze Feedback**: Gather feedback from various sources, such as surveys, reviews, and support interactions. Use AI to analyze this feedback and identify common issues and trends.

- **Enhance Support Processes**: Implement AI tools to improve support processes, such as automated ticketing systems, chatbots, and virtual assistants.

- **Act on Insights**: Use insights from AI analysis to make improvements in service quality, address customer concerns, and enhance the overall experience.

Conclusion

AI is revolutionizing after-sales services in car dealerships by offering advanced solutions for predictive maintenance, upselling, and customer retention. Predictive maintenance helps prevent breakdowns and reduce costs, while AI-driven upselling identifies opportunities for additional sales and enhances the customer experience. Personalized communication and AI-driven support improve customer engagement and satisfaction, leading to increased loyalty and repeat business. By leveraging AI in after-sales services, car dealerships can optimize their operations, strengthen customer relationships, and drive long-term success.

In the next chapter, we will explore how to measure the success of AI-driven marketing efforts, focusing on key performance indicators (KPIs) and metrics for assessing the impact of AI on marketing strategies.

Chapter 12: Measuring Success with AI

In the digital age, measuring the success of marketing efforts is essential for understanding their effectiveness and guiding strategic decisions. Artificial intelligence (AI) enhances the ability to measure and optimize marketing performance by providing advanced analytics, tracking key performance indicators (KPIs), and offering actionable insights. This chapter explores how to measure the success of AI-driven marketing strategies, focusing on KPIs, metrics, and the process of adjusting strategies based on AI insights.

KPIs and Metrics for AI-Driven Marketing

Key performance indicators (KPIs) and metrics are critical for evaluating the success of marketing campaigns and strategies. AI provides sophisticated tools for tracking and analyzing these indicators, enabling dealerships to make data-driven decisions and optimize their marketing efforts.

1. Defining Key Performance Indicators (KPIs)

KPIs are specific, measurable values that indicate the effectiveness of marketing strategies and campaigns. For AI-driven marketing, KPIs should align with the dealership's goals and objectives. Common KPIs for evaluating AI-driven marketing include:

- **Customer Acquisition Cost (CAC)**: The cost associated with acquiring a new customer, including marketing and sales expenses. AI can help track and optimize CAC by analyzing the effectiveness of different marketing channels and strategies.

- **Return on Investment (ROI)**: The financial return generated from marketing investments compared to the cost of those investments. AI can provide insights into which campaigns and channels deliver the highest ROI.

- **Conversion Rate**: The percentage of leads or prospects that convert into customers. AI can help analyze conversion rates across different stages of the customer journey and identify factors influencing conversion.

- **Customer Lifetime Value (CLV)**: The total revenue generated from a customer over their lifetime. AI can assist in predicting CLV based on customer behavior and interactions.

- **Engagement Metrics**: Metrics such as click-through rates (CTR), time spent on site, and social media interactions. AI can analyze engagement metrics to assess the effectiveness of content and campaigns.

- **Lead Quality**: The effectiveness of leads generated by marketing efforts. AI can help evaluate lead quality by analyzing characteristics and behaviors of high-converting leads.

2. Tracking and Analyzing Metrics

AI tools provide advanced capabilities for tracking and analyzing marketing metrics, enabling dealerships to gain deeper insights into their performance. Key steps for tracking and analyzing metrics include:

- **Integrate Data Sources**: Consolidate data from various sources, such as website analytics, CRM systems, and social media platforms. AI can aggregate and analyze data from multiple sources to provide a comprehensive view of marketing performance.

- **Use AI Analytics Platforms**: Leverage AI-powered analytics platforms, such as Google Analytics, Adobe Analytics, or HubSpot, to track and analyze marketing metrics. These platforms offer advanced features such as predictive analytics, segmentation, and reporting.

- **Monitor Performance in Real-Time**: Utilize AI tools to monitor marketing performance in real-time and identify trends or anomalies. Real-time monitoring allows for timely adjustments to optimize campaign effectiveness.

- **Generate Insights**: AI algorithms can generate actionable insights by analyzing patterns and correlations in marketing data. Use these insights to understand the factors driving performance and make informed decisions.

- **Visualize Data**: Present metrics and insights using data visualization tools, such as dashboards and reports. Visual representations of data help stakeholders quickly grasp performance trends and results.

3. Adjusting Strategies Based on AI Insights

AI provides valuable insights that can guide the adjustment and optimization of marketing strategies. To effectively adjust strategies based on AI insights, follow these steps:

- **Identify Areas for Improvement**: Analyze AI-generated insights to identify areas where marketing strategies may need adjustment. Look for trends, patterns, or underperforming elements that require attention.

- **Test and Experiment**: Implement A/B testing and experimentation to evaluate the impact of different strategies and tactics. AI can help analyze the results of these tests and determine which approaches deliver the best outcomes.

- **Optimize Campaigns**: Use AI insights to optimize marketing campaigns by adjusting targeting, messaging, and channel strategies. For example, if AI identifies a high-performing audience segment, focus more resources on targeting that segment.

- **Refine Budget Allocation**: Adjust budget allocation based on AI analysis of campaign performance and ROI. Redirect resources to high-performing channels and strategies to maximize returns.

- **Monitor Impact**: Continuously monitor the impact of adjustments on marketing performance. Use AI tools to track changes in KPIs and metrics and ensure that the adjustments are delivering the desired results.

Conclusion

Measuring the success of AI-driven marketing efforts is essential for optimizing performance and achieving business goals. By defining relevant KPIs, tracking and analyzing metrics, and adjusting strategies based on AI insights, car dealerships can enhance their marketing effectiveness and drive better results. AI provides advanced tools for monitoring performance, generating insights, and making data-driven decisions, enabling dealerships to stay competitive and achieve long-term success.

In the next chapter, we will explore future trends and considerations in AI for car dealership marketing, including emerging technologies and their potential impact on the industry.

Part 4: Future Trends and Considerations

Chapter 13: The Future of AI in Car Dealership Marketing

As technology continues to advance, the role of artificial intelligence (AI) in car dealership marketing is evolving rapidly. The future of AI promises to bring new opportunities, challenges, and innovations that will shape how dealerships engage with customers and drive their marketing strategies. This chapter explores emerging technologies, long-term impacts on the industry, and what dealerships can expect as AI continues to advance.

Emerging Technologies in AI

The landscape of AI is constantly evolving, with new technologies and applications emerging that can significantly impact car dealership marketing. Staying informed about these developments can help dealerships remain competitive and leverage the latest advancements to enhance their strategies.

1. Generative AI

Generative AI refers to AI systems that can create new content, such as text, images, and videos, based on input data. This technology has the potential to revolutionize marketing by enabling the creation of personalized and dynamic content at scale.

Applications in Car Dealership Marketing

Dynamic Content Creation: Generative AI can create personalized marketing materials, such as email templates, social media posts, and advertisements, tailored to individual customer preferences and behaviors.

Virtual Test Drives and Showrooms: Generative AI can enhance virtual test drives and showrooms by creating realistic and interactive simulations of vehicles and driving experiences.

Content Generation for SEO: AI-generated content can improve search engine optimization (SEO) efforts by producing high-quality and relevant content that attracts and engages potential customers.

2. AI-Driven Augmented Reality (AR)

Augmented reality (AR) overlays digital information onto the real world, creating interactive and immersive experiences. AI-driven AR can enhance marketing efforts by providing customers with engaging and informative visualizations.

Applications in Car Dealership Marketing

Interactive Vehicle Visualization: AI-powered AR can allow customers to visualize how different vehicle models, colors, and features will look in real-world environments, enhancing their decision-making process.

Virtual Showroom Enhancements: AR can enhance virtual showrooms by providing interactive elements, such as virtual vehicle walkthroughs, feature demonstrations, and customization options.

AR-Based Advertising: AR can be used in advertising campaigns to create engaging and interactive experiences that capture customers' attention and drive interest.

3. Advanced Natural Language Processing (NLP)

Natural language processing (NLP) enables AI systems to understand and generate human language. Advanced NLP technologies can improve customer interactions and enhance marketing efforts through more sophisticated and natural language capabilities.

Applications in Car Dealership Marketing

Enhanced Chatbots and Virtual Assistants: NLP can improve the functionality of chatbots and virtual assistants by enabling them to understand and respond to complex customer inquiries with greater accuracy.

Sentiment Analysis: NLP can analyze customer feedback, reviews, and social media interactions to gauge sentiment and identify trends, helping dealerships understand customer perceptions and preferences.

Content Creation: NLP can assist in generating high-quality content, such as blog posts, product descriptions, and marketing copy, by understanding context and producing relevant text.

Long-Term Impact on the Industry

The integration of AI into car dealership marketing will have a profound and lasting impact on the industry. Understanding these long-term effects can help dealerships prepare for future developments and adapt their strategies accordingly.

1. Transformation of Customer Expectations

As AI technologies advance, customer expectations will continue to evolve. Dealerships will need to adapt to these changing expectations by providing increasingly personalized, convenient, and engaging experiences.

Impact on Customer Expectations

Higher Personalization: Customers will expect highly personalized interactions and offers based on their preferences and behaviors. Dealerships will need to leverage AI to deliver tailored experiences that meet these expectations.

Increased Convenience: AI-driven solutions, such as virtual showrooms and automated customer support, will set new standards for convenience and accessibility. Dealerships will need to embrace these technologies to remain competitive.

Enhanced Engagement: Customers will seek more interactive and immersive experiences, such as AI-powered AR and virtual test drives. Dealerships will need to invest in innovative technologies to engage customers effectively.

2. Evolution of Marketing Strategies

AI will continue to drive changes in marketing strategies, leading to more data-driven, efficient, and effective approaches. Dealerships will need to adapt their strategies to leverage the latest AI advancements and stay ahead of the competition.

Impact on Marketing Strategies

Data-Driven Decision Making: AI will enable more precise and data-driven decision-making, allowing dealerships to optimize their marketing strategies based on real-time insights and analytics.

Automated Campaign Management: AI-powered tools will automate various aspects of campaign management, including targeting, bidding, and optimization, leading to more efficient and effective marketing efforts.

Enhanced Measurement and Analytics: AI will improve the accuracy and depth of marketing measurement and analytics, providing dealerships with more comprehensive insights into campaign performance and customer behavior.

3. Ethical and Regulatory Considerations

As AI becomes more prevalent in marketing, ethical and regulatory considerations will play an increasingly important role. Dealerships will need to navigate these challenges to ensure responsible and compliant use of AI technologies.

Impact on Ethics and Regulation

Data Privacy: The use of AI in marketing involves the collection and analysis of customer data. Dealerships will need to ensure compliance with data privacy regulations and implement measures to protect customer information.

Transparency and Fairness: AI algorithms should be transparent and fair, avoiding biases and ensuring equitable treatment of all customers. Dealerships will need to address ethical considerations and promote fairness in AI-driven marketing practices.

Regulatory Compliance: As AI technologies evolve, new regulations and guidelines may be introduced. Dealerships will need to stay informed about regulatory changes and adapt their practices to comply with legal requirements.

Preparing for the Future

To prepare for the future of AI in car dealership marketing, dealerships should:

Invest in Emerging Technologies: Stay informed about emerging AI technologies and consider investing in those that align with your marketing goals and objectives.

Adapt to Changing Customer Expectations: Continuously monitor and adapt to evolving customer expectations by leveraging AI to provide personalized, convenient, and engaging experiences.

Embrace Data-Driven Strategies: Utilize AI to drive data-driven decision-making and optimize marketing strategies based on real-time insights and analytics.

Address Ethical and Regulatory Challenges: Implement measures to ensure ethical and compliant use of AI technologies, including data privacy, transparency, and fairness.

Conclusion

The future of AI in car dealership marketing is bright, with emerging technologies and advancements promising to transform the industry. By staying informed about the latest developments, adapting to changing customer expectations, and addressing ethical and regulatory considerations, dealerships can leverage AI to enhance their marketing efforts and drive long-term success. Embracing AI will enable dealerships to stay competitive, deliver exceptional experiences, and thrive in an increasingly digital and data-driven world.

In the next chapter, we will explore the ethical considerations and challenges associated with AI in marketing, focusing on data privacy, fairness, and responsible use of technology.

Chapter 14: Ethical Considerations and Challenges

As artificial intelligence (AI) becomes increasingly integrated into car dealership marketing, ethical considerations and challenges come to the forefront. The use of AI introduces various complexities related to data privacy, fairness, transparency, and the responsible use of technology. This chapter explores these ethical considerations, offering insights and guidelines for dealerships to navigate the evolving landscape of AI with integrity and accountability.

Data Privacy and Security

One of the primary ethical concerns with AI in marketing is data privacy. AI systems often rely on vast amounts of customer data to function effectively, raising questions about how this data is collected, stored, and used.

1. **Ensuring Data Privacy**
   - **Data Collection Practices**: Dealerships should adopt transparent data collection practices, informing customers about what data is collected, how it is used, and obtaining explicit consent. Clear privacy policies and user agreements are essential.

   - **Data Minimization**: Collect only the data necessary for achieving marketing goals. Avoid excessive data collection that could pose unnecessary risks to customer privacy.

   - **Data Protection**: Implement robust security measures to protect customer data from unauthorized access, breaches, and misuse. Use encryption, secure storage solutions, and access controls to safeguard sensitive information.

- **Compliance with Regulations**: Adhere to data privacy regulations such as the General Data Protection Regulation (GDPR) in Europe, the California Consumer Privacy Act (CCPA) in the United States, and other relevant laws. Ensure that AI practices align with legal requirements for data protection and privacy.

2. Transparency in Data Use
    - **Informing Customers**: Clearly communicate how customer data will be used in AI-driven marketing efforts. Provide transparency regarding data usage, including any third parties involved in processing or analyzing the data.

    - **User Control**: Allow customers to manage their data preferences and opt-out options. Provide mechanisms for users to access, correct, or delete their data if desired.

    - **Accountability**: Establish accountability mechanisms for data handling practices. Designate personnel or teams responsible for overseeing data privacy and security.

Responsible Use of Technology

The responsible use of AI involves ethical decision-making, transparency, and accountability in technology deployment and marketing practices.

1. Ethical Decision-Making
    - **Aligning with Values**: Ensure that AI-driven marketing practices align with the dealership's values and ethical standards. Make decisions that prioritize customer well-being and trust.

    - **Ethical AI Design**: Design AI systems with ethical considerations in mind. Incorporate principles of fairness, transparency, and accountability into the development and implementation of AI technologies.

- **Continuous Evaluation**: Regularly evaluate AI practices and their impact on customers. Stay informed about emerging ethical issues and adapt practices to address new challenges.

2. Transparency and Communication
- **Clear Communication**: Communicate transparently with customers about AI use in marketing. Explain how AI enhances their experience and address any concerns they may have.

- **Educating Stakeholders**: Educate internal teams, partners, and stakeholders about ethical AI practices. Promote awareness of ethical considerations and foster a culture of responsibility.

- **Reporting and Accountability**: Establish mechanisms for reporting and addressing ethical concerns related to AI. Create accountability structures to ensure that ethical standards are upheld.

Conclusion

Ethical considerations and challenges are integral to the responsible use of AI in car dealership marketing. By addressing data privacy, fairness, and the responsible use of technology, dealerships can ensure that their AI practices align with ethical standards and foster trust with customers. Transparent communication, inclusive strategies, and ethical decision-making are key to navigating the complexities of AI and maintaining a positive relationship with customers. As AI continues to evolve, dealerships must remain vigilant and adaptable, prioritizing ethics and responsibility in their marketing efforts.

In the next chapter, we will explore how to build an AI-ready team, focusing on skills, training, and integrating AI into company culture.

Chapter 15: Building an AI-Ready Team

As artificial intelligence (AI) becomes increasingly integral to car dealership marketing, building an AI-ready team is crucial for leveraging the technology effectively. An AI-ready team not only possesses the necessary skills and expertise but also embraces a culture that fosters innovation and adaptability. This chapter outlines the key components of building such a team, including skills and training, integrating AI into company culture, and strategies for ongoing development and collaboration.

Skills and Training

Developing an AI-ready team requires a blend of technical, analytical, and strategic skills. Investing in the right training and professional development ensures that team members can effectively use AI tools and contribute to successful marketing strategies.

1. Identifying Key Skills

To effectively implement and manage AI in marketing, team members should possess a range of skills, including:

- **Data Analysis**: Proficiency in analyzing and interpreting data is essential. Team members should be skilled in using data analytics tools and techniques to derive insights from AI-generated data.

- **AI and Machine Learning**: Understanding AI and machine learning concepts, including algorithms, models, and applications, is crucial. Knowledge of how AI systems are developed and how they function can help in implementing and optimizing AI solutions.

- **Digital Marketing**: Familiarity with digital marketing strategies and tools is important. Team members should understand how AI can enhance various aspects of digital marketing, such as SEO, content creation, and customer engagement.

- **Technical Skills**: Skills in programming languages (e.g., Python, R) and familiarity with AI development frameworks (e.g., TensorFlow, PyTorch) can be beneficial for those involved in developing or customizing AI solutions.

- **Project Management**: Effective project management skills are needed to oversee AI initiatives, coordinate with different teams, and ensure that projects are completed on time and within budget.

2. Providing Training and Development

Investing in training and development helps team members acquire and enhance the skills necessary for working with AI. Consider the following approaches:

- **Training Programs**: Enroll team members in training programs and courses focused on AI, data science, and digital marketing. Online platforms, universities, and industry organizations often offer relevant courses and certifications.

- **Workshops and Seminars**: Host workshops and seminars to provide hands-on experience with AI tools and technologies. These events can also serve as opportunities to learn from industry experts and peers.

- **Continuous Learning**: Encourage a culture of continuous learning by providing access to resources such as industry publications, research papers, and online tutorials. Stay updated on the latest AI trends and advancements.

- **Cross-Training**: Facilitate cross-training opportunities where team members can learn about different aspects of AI and digital marketing. This approach promotes a well-rounded understanding of AI applications and fosters collaboration.

Integrating AI into Company Culture

Building an AI-ready team involves more than just technical skills; it requires integrating AI into the company culture and fostering an environment that supports innovation and collaboration.

1. Promoting a Culture of Innovation
- **Encourage Experimentation**: Foster a culture where experimentation and innovation are encouraged. Allow team members to explore new AI technologies, test hypotheses, and develop creative solutions.

- **Celebrate Successes**: Recognize and celebrate successes and milestones achieved through AI initiatives. Acknowledge the contributions of team members and share successes with the broader organization.

- **Support Continuous Improvement**: Emphasize the importance of continuous improvement and adaptation. Encourage team members to seek feedback, learn from experiences, and apply insights to enhance AI strategies.

2. Facilitating Collaboration and Communication
- **Cross-Functional Teams**: Create cross-functional teams that include members from marketing, data science, IT, and other relevant departments. Collaboration between different expertise areas ensures that AI initiatives are well-rounded and effective.

- **Clear Communication**: Establish clear communication channels to facilitate information sharing and coordination. Regular meetings, updates, and reporting mechanisms help keep everyone aligned and informed.

- **Knowledge Sharing**: Promote knowledge sharing and collaboration by organizing team discussions, workshops, and internal presentations. Encourage team members to share their insights and experiences with AI.

3. Leadership and Support
    - **Provide Leadership Support**: Ensure that leadership supports and champions AI initiatives. Leadership involvement is crucial for securing resources, aligning strategies, and driving the adoption of AI technologies.

    - **Set Clear Goals and Expectations**: Define clear goals and expectations for AI projects and initiatives. Ensure that team members understand the objectives, key performance indicators, and desired outcomes.

    - **Allocate Resources**: Provide the necessary resources, including technology, tools, and budget, to support AI initiatives. Adequate resources enable teams to implement and manage AI solutions effectively.

Strategies for Ongoing Development and Collaboration

Maintaining an AI-ready team requires ongoing development and collaboration to adapt to evolving technologies and industry trends.

1. **Stay Updated on Industry Trends**
   - **Industry Conferences**: Attend industry conferences and events to stay informed about the latest AI advancements and marketing trends. Networking with peers and experts can provide valuable insights and opportunities.

   - **Professional Associations**: Join professional associations and organizations related to AI, data science, and digital marketing. Membership can provide access to resources, training, and industry updates.

   - **Research and Publications**: Regularly read research papers, industry reports, and publications related to AI and marketing. Stay informed about emerging technologies and best practices.

2. **Foster External Partnerships**
   - **Collaborate with Vendors**: Partner with AI technology vendors and consultants to gain expertise and access to advanced tools. Vendor partnerships can provide support, training, and insights into AI implementation.

   - **Engage with Industry Experts**: Seek guidance and mentorship from industry experts and thought leaders. Engaging with experts can provide valuable perspectives and help address complex challenges.

   - **Participate in Research Projects**: Collaborate on research projects and initiatives related to AI and marketing. Participation in research can offer opportunities to explore new technologies and approaches.

Conclusion

Building an AI-ready team is essential for harnessing the full potential of AI in car dealership marketing. By developing the necessary skills, integrating AI into company culture, and fostering ongoing development and collaboration, dealerships can create a team that drives successful AI initiatives and adapts to evolving technologies. An AI-ready team not only enhances marketing effectiveness but also positions the dealership for long-term success in an increasingly digital and data-driven industry.

Final Conclusion

As the automotive industry continues to evolve, the integration of artificial intelligence (AI) into car dealership marketing presents both exciting opportunities and significant challenges. This book has explored how AI can revolutionize marketing strategies, enhance customer experiences, and drive growth for dealerships. However, embracing AI requires careful consideration of ethical implications, technical skills, and strategic alignment.

Embracing AI for Competitive Advantage

AI offers transformative potential for car dealerships by improving efficiency, personalizing customer interactions, and optimizing marketing efforts. From predictive analytics that refine targeting and personalization to AI-driven chatbots that enhance customer support, the technology enables dealerships to engage more effectively with their audience and make data-driven decisions.

Navigating Ethical Considerations

As with any powerful technology, AI comes with ethical responsibilities. Data privacy and security are paramount, requiring dealerships to implement transparent data practices and robust protection measures. Responsible use of AI involves ongoing commitment to ethical principles, transparency, and accountability.

Building a Future-Ready Team

Successfully leveraging AI requires building an AI-ready team equipped with the right skills, training, and culture. Investing in continuous learning and fostering a culture of innovation are essential for adapting to technological advancements. By promoting cross-functional collaboration and providing leadership support, dealerships can ensure their teams are well-prepared to navigate the evolving landscape of AI.

Preparing for the Future

The future of AI in car dealership marketing is both dynamic and promising. Emerging technologies, such as generative AI and advanced natural language processing, will further enhance marketing capabilities and customer interactions. Staying informed about industry trends, fostering partnerships, and adapting to new developments will help dealerships remain competitive and innovative.

Final Thoughts

The integration of AI into car dealership marketing represents a significant shift towards a more data-driven, personalized, and efficient approach. By understanding and addressing the ethical implications, investing in team development, and embracing technological advancements, dealerships can unlock the full potential of AI and drive meaningful growth.

As you move forward in implementing AI strategies, remember that success lies in the balance of innovation and responsibility. Embrace the opportunities AI offers, but do so with a commitment to ethical practices and a focus on creating value for both your customers and your business.

Thank you for exploring the transformative power of AI in car dealership marketing. May your journey towards innovation and excellence be both rewarding and impactful.

Introduction 1
   (table of contents at the end of the book) 1
   Purpose of the Book 1
   Why Car Dealerships Need AI 2
   Overview of What Readers Will Learn 2
   Part 1: The Basics of Car Dealership Marketing 3
Chapter 1: Understanding the Automotive Market 3
   Market Trends and Consumer Behavior 3
      Key Market Trends 3
      Understanding Consumer Behavior 5
   Traditional vs. Digital Marketing in Car Dealerships 7
      Traditional Marketing Approaches 7
      The Shift to Digital Marketing 7
Chapter 2: The Customer Journey in Automotive Sales 10
   Awareness Stage 10
      Understanding the Awareness Stage 10
      Strategies for the Awareness Stage 10
   Consideration Stage 12
      Understanding the Consideration Stage 12
      Strategies for the Consideration Stage 12
   Decision Stage 14
      Understanding the Decision Stage 14
      Strategies for the Decision Stage 14
   Importance of Customer Experience 15
Chapter 3: Branding and Positioning 17
   Building a Strong Brand Identity 18
      Understanding Brand Identity 18
      Key Components of Brand Identity 18
   Differentiating Your Dealership 20
      The Importance of Differentiation 20
      Strategies for Differentiation 20
   Branding in the Digital Age 23
      Online Presence and Reputation Management 23
   Measuring Brand Success 24

    Key Performance Indicators (KPIs) 24
    Conclusion 26
Chapter 4: Digital Marketing Fundamentals 27
    SEO and Content Marketing 27
        Understanding SEO 27
        Key SEO Strategies for Car Dealerships 27
        Content Marketing for Car Dealerships 31
    Social Media Strategies 33
        The Role of Social Media in Car Dealership Marketing 33
        Key Social Media Platforms for Car Dealerships 33
        Social Media Content Ideas 35
    Email Marketing and CRM Integration 36
        The Power of Email Marketing 36
        Building an Email List 36
        Email Content Strategies 38
        Integrating CRM with Email Marketing 39
    Conclusion 39
Part 2: Integrating AI into Car Dealership Marketing 40
Chapter 5: Introduction to AI in Marketing 40
    What is AI? 41
    Key AI Technologies Relevant to Marketing 42
        1. Machine Learning (ML) 42
        2. Natural Language Processing (NLP) 43
        3. Computer Vision 44
        4. Predictive Analytics 44
        5. Personalization Engines 45
    Benefits of AI in Car Dealership Marketing 45
    Getting Started with AI in Marketing 47
    Conclusion 49
Chapter 6: AI-Driven Customer Insights 49
    Data Collection and Analysis 50
        1. Sources of Customer Data 50
        2. AI-Driven Data Analysis 51
    Predictive Analytics and Personalization 53
        1. Predictive Analytics Applications 53
        2. Personalization Strategies 54

  Enhancing Customer Experience with AI-Driven Insights................ 54
    1. Improving Customer Engagement.. 55
    2. Streamlining the Sales Process... 55
    3. Enhancing Customer Support...55
    4. Building Long-Term Relationships.. 55
  Conclusion... 56
Chapter 7: Chatbots and Virtual Assistants..57
  Enhancing Customer Interaction.. 57
    1. Benefits of Chatbots and Virtual Assistants...................... 58
    2. Common Use Cases for Chatbots in Car Dealerships........... 59
    3. Implementing Effective Chatbots... 59
  Automating Customer Support.. 61
    1. Handling Inquiries and Providing Information......................... 61
    2. Assisting with Troubleshooting... 61
    3. Supporting After-Sales Service...62
    4. Collecting Feedback and Reviews..62
  Conclusion...62
Chapter 8: AI in Advertising and Lead Generation........................... 63
  Programmatic Advertising...64
    1. What is Programmatic Advertising?..64
    2. Benefits of Programmatic Advertising for Car Dealerships.....64
    3. Implementing Programmatic Advertising.............................. 65
  AI-Powered Lead Scoring and Management.................................... 66
    1. What is Lead Scoring?..67
    2. How AI Enhances Lead Scoring... 67
    3. Implementing AI-Powered Lead Scoring............................... 68
  AI in Lead Management..69
    1. Automating Lead Nurturing.. 69
    2. Predicting Lead Behavior..69
    3. Personalizing Communication... 70
    4. Analyzing Lead Data...70
  Conclusion... 71
Chapter 9: AI in Pricing and Inventory Management........................ 72
  Dynamic Pricing Models... 72
    1. What is Dynamic Pricing?... 72
    2. Benefits of AI-Powered Dynamic Pricing................................ 73

    3. Implementing Dynamic Pricing..73
  Inventory Optimization...75
    1. What is Inventory Optimization?..75
    2. Benefits of AI-Powered Inventory Optimization.....................75
    3. Implementing AI-Powered Inventory Optimization................76
  Conclusion...77
Chapter 10: Enhancing the Customer Experience with AI............ 78
  Virtual Showrooms and Test Drives...78
    1. What are Virtual Showrooms?..79
    2. Benefits of Virtual Showrooms...79
    3. Implementing Virtual Showrooms...80
    4. Virtual Test Drives..80
  AI-Enhanced Personalization... 82
    1. Personalized Recommendations..82
    2. AI-Driven Customer Service...83
    3. Tailored Marketing Campaigns.. 84
  Conclusion...84
Chapter 11: AI in After-Sales Services... 85
  Predictive Maintenance and Upselling...86
    1. What is Predictive Maintenance?... 86
    2. Benefits of Predictive Maintenance.. 86
    3. Implementing Predictive Maintenance...................................87
    4. AI-Driven Upselling Opportunities..88
  Customer Retention Strategies..89
    1. Personalized Communication...89
    2. AI-Driven Customer Feedback and Support..........................91
  Conclusion...92
Chapter 12: Measuring Success with AI.. 93
  KPIs and Metrics for AI-Driven Marketing......................................93
    1. Defining Key Performance Indicators (KPIs)......................... 94
    2. Tracking and Analyzing Metrics... 95
    3. Adjusting Strategies Based on AI Insights.............................96
  Conclusion...97
Chapter 14: Ethical Considerations and Challenges.................... 105
  Data Privacy and Security..105
    1. Ensuring Data Privacy.. 105

- 2. Transparency in Data Use 106
- Responsible Use of Technology 107
  - 1. Ethical Decision-Making 107
  - 2. Transparency and Communication 107
- Conclusion 108

Chapter 15: Building an AI-Ready Team **108**
- Skills and Training 109
  - 1. Identifying Key Skills 109
  - 2. Providing Training and Development 110
- Integrating AI into Company Culture 111
  - 1. Promoting a Culture of Innovation 111
  - 2. Facilitating Collaboration and Communication 112
  - 3. Leadership and Support 112
- Strategies for Ongoing Development and Collaboration 113
  - 1. Stay Updated on Industry Trends 113
  - 2. Foster External Partnerships 113
- Conclusion 114

Final Conclusion **115**
- Embracing AI for Competitive Advantage 115
- Navigating Ethical Considerations 115
- Building a Future-Ready Team 116
- Preparing for the Future 116
- Final Thoughts 116